T0385782

The Portrayal of Czechoslovakia in
the American Print Media, 1938-1989

The Portrayal of Czechoslovakia in the American Print Media, 1938-1989

Edited by Gregory C. Ference

East European Monographs, Boulder
Distributed by Columbia University Press, New York
2006

EAST EUROPEAN MONOGRAPHS, NO. DCXCII

Printed in the United States of America

CONTENTS

CHAPTER 1

SHADOWS IN THE SEARCHLIGHT:

AN INTRODUCTION TO AMERICAN MEDIA

COVERAGE OF CZECHOSLOVAKIA

Owen V. Johnson

THE PICTURES remain etched in our historical minds. Young Edward R. Murrow reported for fledgling CBS News the great 1938 European crisis, now referred to as Munich, as Americans gathered around their firesides to listen how the European powers had sliced up Czechoslovakia to ensure "peace in our time." In February 1948, any wavering policymakers of the United States cast aside their doubts about the communist threat after a drunk Prime Minister Klement Gottwald told a frozen throng in Prague's Old Town Square that communism had triumphed in Czechoslovakia.

In 1968, Americans watched transfixed as television showed the tanks of the Soviet Union and four of its satellites rolling across the borders of Czechoslovakia while its citizens passively resisted. In November 1989, the nation viewed with excitement as the famous fabled walls of Berlin came tumbling down. A week later, crowds surged into Prague's Wenceslas Square to shake their keys and bring down the communists.

Although the country was called Czechoslovakia, almost all our reports came from Prague and the Czech Lands of Bohemia and Moravia. Slovakia remained an invisible appendage in the East whose people appeared in American media only as suffixes.

This book examines American print media coverage of the key events in the history of Czechoslovakia from 1938 to 1989. Since

Czechoslovakia disappeared from Western media coverage most of those five decades, this book shows whatever pictures of Czechoslovakia might have been in people's minds during those formidable years of 1938, 1948, 1968, and 1989. It will provide historians of East Central Europe a snapshot of what the world sees when American media's restless searchlight has landed on the "lands between." It offers communication scholars a study of the performance of the print media of the United States over time in their coverage of one country that occasionally has been the center of world attention. This introduction places the study in the context of the history of news and information flows. It sets the scene for the detailed studies that make up the heart of the book.

Conditioned by the apparent affects of propaganda in World War One and in the rise of Adolf Hitler to power in Germany, most Americans in the first half of the twentieth century believed in powerful media effects, much simpler than the 24-hour digitized information and opinion flow of today. The sole sources of radio news in the interwar period were three or four major networks which did not devote much attention to news, let alone international events, until the mid-1930s when the shadows of Hitler and Italian dictator Benito Mussolini spread across Europe.

Newspapers competed vigorously for readers in American cities, but serious international news did not form a basis for that competition. Then, as now, a small handful of American sources maintained correspondents and bureaus overseas. These knowledgeable specialists supplied their home papers with somewhat informed reports about events in the world. More often than not, however, these reporters did not bother to learn the language of the country they covered, except in certain cases such as Paris and Berlin. The correspondents, even though heavily concentrated in Europe, rarely ventured into the geographical territory eventually called "Eastern Europe" during the Cold War. Instead, they looked for sources who spoke English, French or German in order to write their stories.[1] Then and later, these journalists formed the elite of the profession. In his classic study, *The Press & Foreign Policy*, Bernard Cohen described the foreign correspondent as "a cosmopolitan among cosmopolitans, a man in gray flannels who ranks very high in the hierarchy of reporters."[2]

Communist authorities rarely welcomed such Western reporters in East Central Europe during the Cold War, seldom giving permanent accreditation to any. Czechoslovak authorities even arrested and tried William A. Oatis of the Associated Press during the height of Stalinism.[3] Those granted visas for short-term trips found that virtually no one would talk to them. Flora Lewis, who first gained fame for her coverage of the Polish unrest of 1956, and, later, as chief foreign affairs columnist for the *New York Times*, recalled for this author the story of her visit to Romania during the regime of Nicolae Ceauşescu. She had found that a good opening question for a conversation in East Central Europe was, "How are things here?" But when she asked a truckload of Romanians that question, one of them answered, "We're not allowed to tell you."

During the Cold War only Belgrade and Warsaw, modestly demonstrating some distance from the Soviets, regularly allowed Western correspondents to be permanently accredited. CBS, NBC, and ABC could afford to keep only one bureau each open in East Central Europe with journalists not always kept in those offices. Western print reporters used Poland and Yugoslavia as jumping off points to cover events in the rest of the region. During a 1985 visit to Poland, I helped the *Los Angeles Times* correspondent to develop an agenda of stories to try to report during a planned trip to Czechoslovakia. Perhaps more importantly, editors at home also contributed to deciding what comprised news in East Central Europe.[4]

In 1989, when I visited Prague as a scholar studying media transformation in East Central Europe, I found ferment just below the surface clearly indicating change. Invited to speak to a journalism class in the supposedly arch-conservative School of Journalism at Charles University in Prague, I heard one teacher urge his students to ask me any question. One of the first inquired about how the West viewed Václav Havel, the playwright later Czechoslovak and Czech president, but still then a non-entity and even public enemy Number One. When I shared this information in Poland with several foreign correspondents, they expressed virtually no interest. They were not present to see it for themselves, and it was hard for them to go there. The change seemed too subtle for them to justify a trip south.

So when times of crisis came to Czechoslovakia in 1938, 1948, 1968, and 1989, the story fell mostly to "parachute journalists," the reporters who can make their careers by descending on stories at the center of world attention, even though they know little about the context of the events and certainly do not know the language. They take their cues from the prevailing news frames or from the White House/State Department, as well as from fellow correspondents.[5]

Most American newspapers during the time period included in this book relied on the Associated Press (AP) and United Press (UP), the two wire services, for just about the only source of international news, although a few also subscribed to news provided by the *New York Times*, the *Washington Post/Los Angeles Times*, or other syndicates. Many of these papers only devoted a page to non-American news, offering little sustained coverage of anything but coups, earthquakes, and contested elections.[6] In a classic example, one Midwestern city editor at mid-century accepted that his paper should provide some foreign news even when readers did not care; his only concern being that any foreign reports not be included "at the expense of local news."[7] The editors, whose daily interactions have focused on local affairs, are today far too often poorly informed on international matters beyond what they may have learned in high school or college. Any editorials they might have written on international matters rarely venture beyond conventional wisdom. The propaganda battles of the Cold War drew sustenance from the views of those editors, with proponents of Radio Free Europe and Radio Liberty firmly convinced that if only people who lived in communist countries had access to "real" news, they would rise up and throw off their shackles.

The World News Map

After World War Two, international news flow became one of the chief subjects of international communication research, influenced in part by a belief in powerful media effects. The "Big Five" international news agencies (AP, UP later UPI, Reuters, Havas, and TASS) proved to be a particular subject of attention because of the important role they played in providing the bulk of their international news for so many of the world's media.[8] Almost all of the research used content analysis to study foreign reports in the news media, a labor-intensive method of research that has limited the extent of studies.[9] Agenda-setting studies in the 1970s strengthened the emphasis on content analysis under the assumption that content analysis was systematic and objective, and that the public perceived the relative importance of issues through the amount of news devoted to various topics.[10] One recent study shows that the more news coverage a country receives on television, the more likely Americans believe that country as vital to the interests of the United States.[11]

Given Americans' relative ignorance of global affairs, however, agenda-setting probably is less predictive for international stories in which the United States is not directly involved, as has been true in all of the major crises of Czechoslovakia, including those studied in this book, because they lack a relevant frame for American audiences.[12] Equally important in considering the Czechoslovak case is that the incidents stopped short of conflict. In all the events discussed in this book, one side chose not to fight. President Edvard Beneš decided in both 1938 and 1948 to back down, as did the Czechoslovak government in 1968. In 1989, Soviet leader Mikhail Gorbachev would not have supported any efforts by the Communist Party of Czechoslovakia to stay in power. Research suggests that the categories of news coverage with the highest levels of conflict correlate positively with public concern with international problems.[13]

The International Press Institute, in the first major study of international reporting, recognized "imbalanced" news exchanges between developed and developing nations.[14] While Czechoslovakia, having been one of the dozen most industrialized countries of the world in the interwar period, could hardly be called a developing nation, it clearly stood on the periphery after 1945, just like the developing countries. News of the major countries of the world flowed to Czechoslovakia; it sent back little in return.

In 1964, communications expert Wilbur Schramm suggested that news flow among countries was determined by the ownership of news agencies and long-distance telecommunication facilities, and the concentration of wealth, technology, and power in a few highly developed countries.[15] Schramm and other scholars of the time subscribed to the gospel of modernization, the idea that countries should work toward and be helped to improve the economic and social systems to reach the development levels of the West. Peace studies advocate Johan Galtung more directly argued that the inequality of international information resulted from the power relationships between the center and periphery countries, an approach that helps make the picture of news about Czechoslovakia much clearer.[16] A more recent analysis confirms that core nations receive extensive coverage from the media in the United States, while the periphery does not.[17] A more complex study found eleven variables that influence international communication flow, including the volume of international trade, gross national product per capita, population density, distance from the United States, daily newspapers/1000 people, literacy, official language, and foreign stock residing in America.[18]

Clearly, two kinds of factors influenced the structure and flow of news. One consisted of factors external to the news process, such as politics and economics, including government censorship and media ownership.[19] In a study helping to explain the Czechoslovak case, media specialist Al Hester suggested four determinants of information flow, based on these external factors, including the hierarchy of nations (geographic size, population, economic development, and length of existence as a sovereign state), cultural affinities (including shared language, the amounts of migration, intermarriage, travel between countries, and the historical relationships such as mother country-colony status), economic associations between countries (including international trade, the amount of foreign aid, and business investment between countries), and news and information conflicts.[20] While some scholars complained about the politicization of international news research, others welcomed the debate because it forced them to consider carefully the values defining their research. The second element influencing the structure and flow of news consisted of factors inherent in the news that enhanced the event's newsworthiness, especially its relevance to elite countries and elite peoples or to something negative, such as conflict, or simply a story that is exceptional.

During the 1970s, discussions of international news flow gradually became more politicized, culminating in a movement called the New World Information Order.[21] Some media scholars sought to depoliticize the topic by designing their studies more carefully. The most prominent of these efforts, a global project conducted under the aegis of the International Association for Mass Communications Research, involved mass communication researchers in twenty-nine countries who looked at data on news for a two-week period in 1979 in forty newspapers, twenty radio and television organizations, and the major news agencies. This study showed a vast amount and diversity of foreign news about most sections of the world. It suggested that allegations that third world and other periphery countries produced only bad news and violence simply did not stand up. Clearly, the United States and Western Europe dominated the world's news. Third world countries did produce more crisis news because more crises more often occurred there.[22] Except for the Soviet Union, "Eastern" Europe remained almost invisible.

A landmark communications study in 1984, by the late Kyoon Hur, helps connect consideration of the coverage of Czechoslovakia to larger concerns about news and information flows. Hur argued that the main problems of international news flow and coverage studies were differences in concepts and methods. He lamented the lack of theoretical and methodological linkages. He suggested that a distinction be made between international news flow analysis dealing mainly with the volume and direction of news flow and international news coverage analysis focusing on the amount, nature, and type of foreign news disseminated across boundaries.[23]

Hur proposed four categories of international news research, three of which clearly relate to the topic of this book: 1) **Geographic approaches** deal with specific countries or regions, and the extent of coverage. 2) **Media approaches** compare coverage by television, radio, magazines, and newspapers. Television is beyond the ken of this book. The first networks did not archive their evening news programs until August 1968, so they missed the crises of 1938, 1948, and almost entirely the one in 1968. Network radio was important only in 1938, with Murrow and H.V. Kaltenborn reporting Munich, but no complete record of their accounts exist. Thus, it makes sense in a comparative study over time to concentrate on newspapers and magazines since they were a constant in the twentieth century.

Third, **event-oriented approaches** look at how different types of news events have been covered. This book falls squarely in this category. Hur observed that the last theme of **time** has almost never been studied. Such an approach is extraordinarily difficult because of the changing global context and developing information technology. Nonetheless, this book makes some tentative steps in this direction.

A 1987 summary of news flow research divided the subject into just two categories: context-oriented and event-oriented. The context-oriented approach examines the relationships between foreign news coverage and contextual or external factors, such as geographical proximity, political affiliation, economic relations or cultural similarity. The second, which best describes the research undertaken in this book, suggests that characteristics inherent in foreign events, such as the degree of deviance and the negative nature of the events, enhance their newsworthiness.[24]

Journalism professor Leonard Chu argues that which stories get covered is largely a matter of routine. Individual and organizational values play a part in the process of establishing this method. Perhaps the most specific news values are conflict and the unusual, or exceptional, certainly a characteristic of all the events discussed in this book. As a matter of convenience, media organizations have developed systems to gather news in the most efficient ways. Thus, they institutionalized a news net, designed to capture the largest amount of news; if most of it has been in the West, that is where the journalists have been. Part of this relates to the question of sources: those in high places in the West have tended to be the most accessible, a significant factor when Western journalism has followed the conventions of objectivity with spokespeople, who can be amply quoted on the various sides of an issue.[25]

Thus, in spite of the various influences that contribute toward deciding what is news—journalists and their editors are ultimately responsible for news selection. These "gatekeepers" apply a set of norms to their professional practice, although routines of the organization can limit the parameters of choice.[26]

The wealth of what has constituted news over the years since the end of World War Two stands in stark contrast to attention to the audience. Who is it that reads what news and why? It is one thing to know how much news, on which subjects, written in what style, is sent, and quite another to know what is consumed and reactions to what is consumed. Researchers seeking persuasive material about a subject in specific publications will certainly find it in isolation, but that is not how readers saw it at the time. The original mass consumers of those media lived full lives with multiple sources of information and ideas not only on the topic in question, but on many others, including both news and day-to-day interactions with family, friends, and colleagues. Even if we could determine what consumers read, we would also need to ascertain how much of the information they retained in forming their view of the world, and how, in turn, they acted on that information. Some researchers continue to believe in powerful media effects: George Gerbner, a communications professor, who experienced the 1956 revolution in Hungary before immigrating to the United States, feels television has conditioned children by age six, and has an impact on all of us through adulthood.

Very few studies examine the availability of news and information to the elites who formulate policy or the people who influence policymakers. This reflects a bias toward normative assumptions about the place of the news media in a democratic society to provide the news that will make it possible for an informed citizenry actively to make choices and influence a government. Unfortunately, as Willard Bleyer, one of the founders of mass communication studies, wrote years ago, "Such a theory of democracy undoubtedly throws a heavy burden on the individual citizen... [who] does *not* have the time, the ability, or the inclination to devote himself to so tremendous a task."[27] Bleyer worried that because mass-circulation newspapers thrived on sensationalism, "they may be powerful agents for good or for ill in working for peace and mutual understanding or for jealousy, hatred, and misunderstanding between nations."[28]

If the educated class had more influence in the making of foreign policy, it is difficult to reconstruct the universe of publications that the chattering classes read at any particular time. In the nineteenth century, news about Czechs and the Czech Lands rarely appeared in the daily press. By the late nineteenth century, periodicals intended for elite consumption, such as *Nation*, carried more material from the Czech Lands, and increasingly presented it with a Czech, rather than an Austro-German, perspective.[29] The conclusion of an article studying nineteenth-century coverage provides a starting point for this book:

> Because almost no author [before 1914] championed or disparaged the Czech cause on a continuing basis, Bohemia, instead of being the recipient of specific attention, became only a part, even if an integral one, of the larger Austrian question, where something was clearly rotten. A faint, but well-defined image of Bohemia and the Czechs, as well as of Austria, was available in periodicals, and there is some evidence that it had penetrated the minds of the elite, but it had not yet reached the middle class.... Because there was no widely-held opinion about the resolution of these conflicts and because European affairs were still of fairly limited interest for American foreign policy, the field was relatively clear for the work of public diplomacy which [future Czechoslovak President Thomas G.] Masaryk and others engaged in during World War I to help bring about United States support for the freedom and independence of the new state of Czechoslovakia.[30]

An active campaign by Czechs and/or Slovaks in the United States seemed one factor not to have influenced coverage of news of the Czech Lands and Slovakia before World War One. While such endeavors have not been entirely absent, they have not been as powerful in influencing American foreign policy as have been Irish-, Italian-, Polish-, or Jewish-Americans.[31]

Even if the influence of the media is accepted, the question remains whether the influence lies in what is news, the way certain issues are covered, or in the opinions expressed. Who, in turn, framed the news and what were their views? If these matters are studied in a research project, how does one determine what news institutions should be studied? For the public at large, what is the relative importance of newspaper stories *versus* editorial comment? There is also a persistent belief that newspapers reflect public opinion. That is not altogether inaccurate because people are more likely to read a publication whose opinions they share. They can only choose, however, from the publications available.

News About Czechoslovakia
Greg Ference provides a fascinating chapter in this book of American public thinking about the Munich crisis with a creative study of editorials and editorial commentary in a selection of newspapers and magazines of the United States. It is an approach that would not be successful in today's media, but provides a superb window on both the American print media of the late 1930s and the transpiring public debate. In the interwar period, people who thought about media influence on foreign policy focused on two issues: the sway of news sources on foreign policy decision-making and the affect on public opinion. Two German researchers, Paul F. Douglass and Karl Bömer, argued in 1932 that the news media were a key factor in international relations.[32] Leland Stowe, a one-time foreign correspondent for the *New York Herald-Tribune*, expressed his belief that the media had played a crucial role in every international conflict.[33] Journalism professor Reginald Coggeshall more specifically wrote that the news media had strong diplomatic influence.[34]

In a time when elite newspapers such as the *New York Times* were yet not available nationwide, city newspapers still believed they had a responsibility to inform their readers about international affairs, in particular instructing them about how to understand global events. Unlike today, local editorial writers made it their job to stay informed about world and national issues by reading nationally-circulated journals. Ernie Pyle, a Scripps-Howard columnist, who later became famous for his wartime columns from the front, referred frequently in his private letters to his reading of the *New Yorker* and other such magazines.[35] Furthermore, journalists interacted with the other more educated individuals in their communities to increase their knowledge on a particular subject.

Newspapers of the 1930s contained many fewer pages than today, so they devoted smaller amounts of space to stories. As a result, readers turned to the editorial pages for some explanation of how to understand new developments. As Ference shows, often they found interpretations that reflected the political views of the publishers on domestic events.

What makes Ference's chapter particularly interesting is the broad range of sources that he employs. Most historians who use print media to chart public thinking use nationally well-known papers, presuming that they were more likely to influence policymakers in the White House or in Foggy Bottom. By looking more widely, Ference reminds us that those newspapers did not always represent the range of opinion abroad in the United States. Particularly interesting is the way he turns to papers such as the *Salisbury Times* (a daily only since December 1923), the *Honolulu Advertiser*, and the African-American *Pittsburgh Courier*. The small-town papers seem to have been far less inclined to have the United States involve itself in a faraway country. To the often-quoted *Newsweek*, *Time*, and *New Republic*, he adds *Independent Woman* and *National Republic*. He discovers that a publication such as *Life* reminded its readers that before Munich, Czechoslovakia maintained a stronger and better-equipped army than that of the Germans, something too often forgotten in retrospective evaluations of the Munich crisis.

The Roosevelt administration tiptoed around the Munich crisis. The president, well aware of the unpreparedness of the American military to intervene in the crisis, knew he did not have the domestic support to do so. Hence, neither the White House nor the State Department offered a consistent message to editorial writers. As Ference shows, much of the editorial debate focused on the actions of the Czechoslovakia, Great Britain, and France, and much less on the United States, particularly after the signing of the Munich Pact. This resembles the situation in the United States in 1967 and 1968, when President Lyndon B. Johnson had begun to have some doubts about Vietnam and for about twelve months did not follow an aggressive media policy. That opened the door for opponents, particularly the growing number of doves in Congress, to express their views. In 1938, in contrast, no group saw the Munich crisis as a touchstone issue. References to the considerable role of the United States in helping create Czechoslovakia in 1918 remained relatively few, given the general absence of news about the country since that year.

The opinion polls cited by Ference clearly show a public aware of the Munich crisis and some of the choices it involved for the United States. Unfortunately, one cannot determine the degree to which American awareness of the crisis related to the newness of the radio medium, which might have had a considerable impact owing to the impression of actually being where history occurred, and the degree to which people were influenced by what they read in the papers and magazines. Thankfully, Greg Ference shows what people said about these issues.

Many Americans did not yet believe that European events might draw their country into a war. In one of his letters in September 1939, after Nazi Germany had invaded Poland, Ernie Pyle speculated that the United States would be in the war in about two years. About the Munich crisis he wrote nothing.

Paul Kubricht, like Ference using a richly diverse pool of print news media, rightly shows that both the situation in Czechoslovakia in 1948, when the communists seized power, and the way in which the media portrayed the situation, qualitatively differed from 1938. The Munich crisis lasted nearly a month and involved the world powers Great Britain and France. The February coup in Prague involved no Western powers, and largely developed underneath Western radar because other stories, both foreign and domestic, competed for media space. The decision of the Czechoslovak government in the summer of 1947, taken under Soviet pressure, to decline participation in the Marshall Plan, had caught the attention of few Americans. Kubricht therefore has chosen very intelligently to portray the print media's picture of Czechoslovakia by focusing on four themes, since a chronology would not be very useful. Only the *New York Times* seems to have had a correspondent based in Prague. Other journalists on the scene had little or no understanding of the developing situation and very few sources. The division within the Czechoslovak cabinet and the failing health of President Beneš meant that no government office actively put forward the government's view of affairs. Not surprisingly, Western reporters had no access to either the Czech and Slovak communists, or their Soviet advisors.

On the other hand, elite knowledge of Czechoslovakia in the United States had improved substantially since 1938. Czechoslovakia had been one of the captive nations of Hitler's Germany during the war. The military, as part of its wartime activities, had created a corps of non-native Czech and Slovak speaking Americans, and an American army, led by General George S. Patton, had liberated the western slice of Czechoslovakia in 1945. During the course of the war, American reporters had made contact and became acquainted with individual Czechoslovak leaders, for example Beneš and especially the jovial diplomat Jan Masaryk, son of the first Czechoslovak president Thomas G. Masaryk, contributing to the strengthening of one theme: ties with the United States that had virtually disappeared during the Munich crisis.

The developing Cold War had encouraged opinion leaders at least to learn something about the geography of East Central Europe. Nonetheless, White Anglo-Saxon Protestants still managed the foreign policy of the United States, and they expressed little warmth toward the region.

As Kubricht properly shows, American portrayal of Czechoslovakia in the print media owed much to domestic political predispositions. These attitudes extended into the United States government as well. Diplomat George F. Kennan, for instance, had warned Secretary of State George C. Marshall that European economic integration would cost the West Czechoslovakia:

> If he ever read the warning I submitted to him in the autumn of 1947 to the effect that the Communists would inevitably crack down on Czechoslovakia in case the effort toward a European recovery program proceeded successfully, I am sure he had forgotten it by the end of February 1948....The greatest mystery of my own role in Washington...was why so much attention was paid in certain instances...and so little in others. The only answer could be that Washington's reactions were deeply subjective, influenced more by domestic-political moods and institutional interests than by any theoretical considerations of our international position.[36]

As had been the case in 1938, Washington had not articulated a clear policy it sought to convey to journalists, in part because no foreign policy goals had been precisely defined. Journalist Joseph C. Harsch observed that by the end of 1947, four different goals were evident: international cooperation built on collective security; a three-power world (US, USSR, and Western Europe); a two-power world (US and USSR); and armed isolation. "The list of inconsistencies in actions and in trends in Washington is a long and disturbing one," he put it bluntly.[37]

American public opinion after the February coup showed an acquiescence in a tension-filled world. More than three quarters of Americans believed war likely within twenty-five years, and that the Soviet Union sought to become the dominant global power. Seventeen percent said the United States should go to war and twenty-seven percent suggested that the country prepare to fight by building up its armed forces. These numbers represent the highest percentages between World War Two and the Korean War.[38]

Nevertheless, of the four years examined in this book, American print media attention to Czechoslovakia was the weakest in 1948. Part of this can be explained by the context of competing stories and inaccessible sources. But the sad reality shows that almost no reporter had the language or area knowledge to report the Czechoslovak situation thoroughly. From Kubricht's account, the Slovak side of the story, including the "practice coup" in November 1947, was almost completely absent from the news coverage.

During the Cold War, American newspapers made sure that their correspondents in key locations overseas, like Moscow, Beijing, Bonn, and Paris, had the requisite area and language training. Such had not been the case with almost every other non-English speaking country in the world, including Czechoslovakia. News executives pointed out that they could not afford to train journalists who stayed in one location for a maximum of three years. They did not want their reporters to become "domesticated." Curiously enough, however, journalists from other countries, such as Germany and France, did not seem to have had the problem of finding language and country-knowledgeable reporters.

American knowledge about Czechoslovakia and the other East Central European countries increased significantly between 1948 and 1968. The United States government invested in graduate programs that trained scholars in East Central European knowledge and languages. The foreign policy and intelligence offices employed hundreds of specialists to analyze and evaluate the happenings in the region.

James Peterson, a political scientist, takes advantage of the social science tradition of content analysis to offer perspectives on 1968 and 1989 that differ substantially from the earlier chapters. Owing to the labor-intensive quality of content analysis and to the distinctly larger amount of material available in 1968, he is only able to look at three newspapers of distinctly different type: the *New York Times*, a newspaper of record; the *Wall Street Journal*, focused on business and economics; and the *Christian Science Monitor*, which most readers used as a supplemental newspaper.

The Iron Curtain denied American reporters most access to Czechoslovakia after 1948. Media institutions of the United States reacted slowly when conditions began to change in the 1960s, largely for administrative reasons. The prohibitive cost of opening new bureaus made it unlikely that newspapers would move reporters into a liberalizing Czechoslovakia until the change had become dramatic.

Editorial managers, particularly foreign editors, make such decisions. As employees in their home offices, they are aware of and subject to the pressing "local" demands of their papers. Intellectual shifts and modest liberalization in Czechoslovakia did not provide these people with the kinds of arguments that would add new foreign correspondents, especially when attention in the United States focused on Vietnam and the Civil Rights Movement. In the American perspective, the whole world concentrated on the Democratic National Convention in Chicago in August 1968, not the Soviet invasion of Czechoslovakia.

Specialized publications such as *East Europe* and the many series from Radio Free Europe made it clear to area specialists already by 1967 that dramatic change was underway in Czechoslovakia, especially in the area of literary and economic freedoms. Substantial national unrest flooded through Slovakia, but even specialist publications did not know of its depth because they were primarily staffed by émigré Czechs or émigré Slovaks strongly committed to the Czechoslovak idea of a country of one people: the Czechoslovaks.

The threat of a Soviet invasion provided the focus that domestic editors in the United States needed to direct attention to Czechoslovakia, as Peterson's data on the chronology of the publishing of stories about Czechoslovakia clearly demonstrate. Well-established American correspondents in Moscow, whose positions stood generally higher than anyone reporting from Prague, confirmed that threat thereby tending to increase the focus on the potential armed conflict.

Peterson's data only show what was published. They cannot portray the topics to which foreign editors and reporters did not direct attention. It might be argued, however, that the constant emphasis in schools and political rhetoric about the evil of communism made it extraordinarily difficult for journalists to pitch stories that suggested a "reform" of communism. The ideological spectrum allowed for communists and anti-communists; reform communism must have struck some editors as an oxymoron.

Once again in 1968, the United States did not have a vital interest in Czechoslovakia. As long as the Soviet bloc did not attempt to expand, the United States could live with it. The White House/State Department, concerned about domestic unrest related to Vietnam, had almost no goals in regard to Czechoslovakia, so found no reason to lead the press in one way or another. Without direction, the correspondents gravitated to the pack, which had fastened onto the story of potential, and then actual, invasion. After the assault, the foreign reporters gradually began to leave Prague because American interest had died out, and Czechoslovak police and party authorities increased the pressure on the correspondents.

Peterson's analysis of coverage of the death throes of communism in Czechoslovakia in 1989 shows a distinctly different picture. He attributes this largely to the general collapse of communism in "Eastern" Europe that year. The liberation of Czechoslovakia from communism became just another chapter. More interesting things had already occurred in Warsaw, Budapest, and Belgrade.

The month-by-month coverage of events shows this most clearly. The overwhelming majority of the news falls in the months of November and December. While significant things took place in Czechoslovakia earlier in the year, they paled in contrast, for example, to the debates, discussions, and elections in Poland.

Twenty years of only short visits by correspondents to Czechoslovakia had prevented them from nurturing a range of sources for information. They could not recognize that a generation of young people had grown up after the Soviet invasion who did not believe in communism or any of its promises. This generation maintained more interest in reading *Burda*, the West German fashion magazine imported by the authorities to try to satisfy the disenchanted population. Reporters did not know that forty percent of the populace could watch foreign television. They were also unaware that the Communist party itself had lost its sense of direction, and found itself unable to formulate and execute reform plans, even when prodded by Moscow.

The content analysis of 1989 shows a much wider range of print media involvement in foreign correspondence. Most of the differences among the newspapers reflect the extent to which those papers had correspondents based in East Central Europe, the quality of these journalists, and the amount of attention they paid to events in Czechoslovakia. The *Los Angeles Times*, for instance, as part of its effort to establish itself as a national paper, had invested heavily in foreign news coverage, including a major bureau in Warsaw that had been monitoring developments in Prague. While many of the correspondents did not come to Prague until November, they had considerable regional experience, and thus brought much more knowledge to their stories than had been the case in the three other crises studied in this book, which helps explain the diversity and range of stories that appeared in the papers.[39]

Once again, the United States, while pleased with the events in Czechoslovakia, had not yet defined any additional goals. Questions about an expanded Europe that might include the Czechs and the Slovaks had not been discussed, which gave the reporters *carte blanche* to develop their stories. While the spotlight remained on East Central Europe, Americans had the best reporting ever, or, are likely to see from this area in the future. Since 1989, the news spotlight has turned away. Today the Czech Republic and Slovakia have become ordinary states, and are of no more interest to foreign correspondents than Spain and Ireland.

Political cartoons in the United States have rarely been studied because it requires not only a knowledge of the incidents being portrayed, but the nature of newspapers at the time, as well as the contemporary approach of cartoonists. Too often cartoons have functioned as a blunt instrument, rather than a sharp commentary. On a day-to-day basis, news cartoons have reflected conservatizing values, rather than a liberal outlook. As historian Mark Summers comments,

> [N]ewspapers are businesses and...an artist representing such institutions will reflect a business perspective....Cartoonists do not simply comment upon events; they are confined by them and compelled to react to them instantly. They are also confined by the restrictions on their medium of expression: the momentary attention that their readers can give, the limitations in the knowledge that readers bring to bear on the subject, and the interest they take in the topic at all.[40]

By presenting in this book a series of American political cartoons about Czechoslovakia, Ference and Kubricht have done a noble service. Too often when we look back historically, we see only the iconic cartoons—such as the *Washington Post*'s Herblock cartoon showing the Lincoln Memorial statue with its head in its hands after the assassination of President John F. Kennedy—and we do not get a sense of what newspaper readers daily saw. Given the relatively limited views of the editorialists, the cartoonists had relatively little material to work with. Their creations did not offer different perspectives, but only illustrated what had already been said, the only exception between the pathetically absurd *Chicago Tribune* cartoon that tried to relate the 1938 Munich crisis to that year's National League pennant race (see Figure 4, Chapter 6). Viewers of these cartoons will also be struck by the way in which cartoonists make Czechoslovak crises into simply Czech ones.

Nearly a century ago, newspaperman Walter Lippmann, in a critical evaluation of the role of the people in a democratic society, observed that

> The press is no substitute for institutions. It is like the beam of a searchlight that moves restlessly about, bringing one episode and then another out of darkness into vision. Men cannot do the work of the world by this light alone. They cannot govern society by episodes, incidents, and eruptions. It is only when they work by a steady light of their own, that the press, when it is turned upon them, reveals a situation intelligible enough for a popular decision.[41]

Lippmann's unpromising perspective offered little hope that readers would be able to make sense of things very often. On four occasions in the twentieth century, the spotlight settled briefly on Czechoslovakia. On three occasions the limelight provided American citizens with a somewhat shadowy picture of the events, but could not agree on what it meant. On the fourth occasion the footprint of a larger spotlight shone on all of East Central Europe bringing the Czechs, but not the Slovaks, into sharper focus. Now that emphasis has moved.

Czechs and Slovaks might hope that the spotlight would never return, because its absence suggests a degree of normalcy. From time to time a story will still break through, such as news that Slovakia expects by 2008 to be the leading producer of cars per capita in the world. Otherwise life goes on.

Thanks to the authors of this book for having helped Americans understand not only how the print media in the United States functioned in their covering of one country in the twentieth century, but also for showing the picture that the media painted.

CHAPTER 2

AMERICAN PRINT MEDIA PERCEPTIONS OF

THE 1938 MUNICH CRISIS

Gregory C. Ference

THE AMERICAN VIEWING PUBLIC in over 5,000 movie houses across the United States began watching the latest release of the quasi-newsreel *The March of Time* entitled "Prelude to Conquest," on September 2, 1938. *Time* magazine's prophetic short film reached over 12 million viewers who saw German dictator Adolf Hitler, with Austria now part of Germany, looking toward Czechoslovakia. Using the Sudeten Germans as a pretext for territorial gain, the Nazis mobilized while Czechoslovak President Edvard Beneš rejected German demands.[1] Unaware of it, the viewing public had just seen a mini-version of the month's upcoming events. Although *The March of Time* dramatized world events, it, along with other newsreels and radio broadcasts, were the principal sources of news for illiterate and semi-illiterate Americans, the former group comprising an estimated 2.9 percent of the population in the 1940 census.[2]

As for literate American, the possibility of a European war developing over the German-Czechoslovak controversy quickly became a well-discussed and much debated topic of interest in the United States. When the American Institute of Public Opinion, or Gallup Poll, surveyed the American public in December 1938, for the "Most Interesting News Event of 1938," the Munich crisis, or as the institute called it, "Czechoslovakia war crisis," received the highest ranking with 23%, nearly double the next largest named topic percentage out of a total of eleven named events.[3] To give an idea of public interest concerning the topic beyond the abundance of material presented in newspapers, a quick glance at the *Reader's Guide to Periodical Literature* under the heading of "Czechoslovakia" lists more than 100 articles pertaining to the crisis, while the heading "Munich four power agreement" produced over fifty in popular magazines in 1938, and 1939.[4]

Methodology

This study does not attempt to be all inclusive of the American print media nor of the opinions of the people of the United States since it examines the issue of the Munich crisis by covering selected journals and newspapers. Nor does this commentary seek to cover the major European events in 1938, leading to the Munich Agreement, although some discussions of the incidents in September 1938 are necessary for context. Rather, it examines how the print media in the United States, largely through newspaper editorials and magazine articles, viewed the occurrences a continent away.

The newspapers covered represent a daily regional sampling: *New York Times* and *Baltimore Sun* for the East; *Chicago Tribune* for the Midwest; *New Orleans Times-Picayune* for the South, and *Los Angeles Times* for the West. The *Honolulu Advertiser* and *Salisbury Times* (Salisbury, Maryland) present a territorial and a local perspective respectively. Together these papers enjoyed a daily circulation figure of over 1.8 million copies in 1938. The popular journals or magazines included in this study are national in scope: *Life, New Republic, Newsweek, New Yorker,* and *Time* whose subscription/publication numbers totaled over two million per issue for 1938. For the non-traditional American print media, this piece looks at the nationwide, weekly African-American newspaper *Pittsburgh Courier*; the five day a week financial newspaper *Wall Street Journal* published by the Dow Jones Company in New York; *Independent Woman,* a monthly magazine issued by the National Federation of Business and Professional Women's Clubs which promoted ideas aimed toward women's equality while reporting news of women's contributions in numerous fields; and *National Republic,* an extreme conservative monthly magazine. These four periodicals had circulation figures close to 250,000 copies for 1938. The total circulation of these papers and periodicals add up to over 4.2 million copies, but this fails to show the totality of the reading public since each copy usually had multiple readers.[5] Nonetheless, the views of the print media discussed here can be divided into three broad groups: isolationist, interventionist, and some combination of the two. Such sentiments mirrored the divisions in the public's response to the developing war clouds in Europe and Asia during the 1930s that culminated in World War Two.

This piece focuses, for the most part, on September and early October 1938, and the explosive situation that resulted in the anti-climatic four-power dictate in late September 1938. The Munich crisis, however, includes other events prior to this period. These begin in the spring with the German annexation of Austria or *Anschluss* in mid-March, allowing Germany to envelop Czechoslovakia on three sides; Sudeten Nazi leader Konrad Henlein's April Karlsbad Program demanding complete autonomy for the German speaking areas of Czechoslovakia, a reconfiguration of the country into a confederation of nationalities, and a pro-German Czechoslovak foreign policy; the late May mobilization of the Czechoslovak military after rumors spread of an impending German invasion; and intermittent clashes between Sudeten Germans and Czechs in the border regions. Other events of significance include the unsuccessful fact-finding mission of British Lord Walter Runciman to mediate the Sudeten dispute which issued its report in early August in favor of the Sudeten Germans; large-scale German army maneuvers that occurred in mid-August; and Admiral Miklós Horthy's state visit to Berlin in late August, who, as regent of Hungary, also had territorial designs on Czechoslovakia.

The Crisis

As the *Reader's Guide* and journalistic coverage amply prove, the crisis soon became a main topic of interest to be watched closely. At the beginning of September, both the *New York Times* and the *Honolulu Advertiser* noted the tenseness in Europe over events in Czechoslovakia. The New York paper indicated that larger issues than just Czechoslovakia were at stake,[6] including the Spanish Civil War and Japanese aggression in China where the Japanese military had been seizing large sections of that country since the early 1930s. Almost a world away from the events, the *Honolulu Advertiser*, although a member of the United Press, gave excellent European coverage seemingly out of proportion to its location in relation to the Pacific and Asia. Perhaps this is due in part to the news editor Jan Jabulka, a Czech-American who moved from Chicago to Hawaii in 1928.[7] In its editorial entitled "Stuff That Makes War," the Hawaiian newspaper offered an interesting observation. Germany claimed to speak on behalf of all Germans outside Germany, hence the problems in Czechoslovakia. If Germany could do so, then the same absurd principle would then hold true for the diaspora of any nation: for example, Sweden in Minnesota, France in Louisiana, Mexico in Texas, and most importantly for Hawaii, Japan. Such mistaken ideals, it concluded, created war. The paper's editorial hoped "Der Fuhrer" would exhaust his pent-up frenzy over the Sudeten issue at the upcoming Nazi Party Congress, thereby calming down and letting the crisis pass without conflict.[8]

In early September, Czechoslovak officials and representatives of the Sudeten Germans discussed Prague's proposals for its German minority while the Sudetens insisted on the adoption of the earlier Karlsbad Program. The *Los Angeles Times* observed that the Prague government was "willing to go to great lengths to appease the German population." If Czechoslovakia granted these terms, the daily speculated, it could cause internal unrest with its own Slavic majority who would view the concessions as surrendering too much.[9] The *New Orleans Times-Picayune* agreed. These demands, if met, would accord Sudeten Germans greater rights than those enjoyed by the Slavs in the country. This was ironic since Nazi Germany backed the Sudetens while denying its own ethnic minorities and non-Nazi party followers basic rights.[10] Noting this contradiction, a week later the Los Angeles daily remarked that if Henlein had been the leader of a Czech minority in Germany, the Nazis would have long ago sent him to a concentration camp or executed him.[11] The *Baltimore Sun* warned that Czechoslovakia's acceptance of the Karlsbad Program pressed by Hitler and Henlein would produce a radical reconfiguring of the country, producing a "Trojan Horse" scenario allowing German influence to inundate the country thereby destroying it. Whether the Czechoslovaks would grant concessions or the Germans would back away from their intransigence, the paper predicted these questions would be answered in the coming weeks.[12] The *Los Angeles Times* believed the upcoming Nazi Party Congress in Nuremberg could answer these questions. It expected that Hitler, who the daily rightly predicted would save his address for the last day of the meeting, might make an important announcement concerning the Sudeten issue. Yet, the paper vacillated in writing that the Führer might say nothing about the problems in Czechoslovakia except to claim in an off-handed manner that Germany had a right to protect Germans everywhere.[13]

For many, the six-day Nazi Party Congress held the key to the resolution of the Sudeten issue. Vera Micheles Dean, a respected specialist in international affairs and research director of the Foreign Policy Association,[14] also believed that the problems between Germany and Czechoslovakia would reach its apex during the Nuremberg party congress. Her article, "EUROPE wants PEACE," published in the September issue of *Independent Woman* before the crisis heated up, accurately described the situation as a "tense curtain raiser for another World War." She characterized British and French friendship as not an aggressive force in foreign affairs, but as a cornerstone of "appeasement" in Europe. Although the two countries had declared their support for Czechoslovakia, they held different viewpoints in relation to it. France was not willing to appease Germany over Czechoslovakia because this would allow German domination of the continent. On the other hand, Great Britain, unprepared for war, feared German strength and urged the Czechoslovaks to grant concessions even though this might allow Nazi hegemony in Europe.[15] Here one finds the first use of the word "appeasement" in the sources consulted to describe Britain's and France's policy toward Nazi aggression prior to the outbreak of the Second World War.

The Nazi Party Congress began in Nuremberg on September 6, but several days earlier, President Beneš had met in Prague with two officials of the Sudeten German party. During their discussions, the Czechoslovak leader took out a piece of paper, and placed it before the Sudeten Germans stating, "Please write your Party's full demands.... I promise you in advance to grant them immediately." When the Sudetens failed to respond, Beneš drafted the so-called "Fourth Plan" in which Czechoslovakia agreed to virtually every point of the April Karlsbad Program.[16] The shocked Sudeten German leaders submitted the plan to their party on September 7, but under orders from Berlin, they used a minor incident, where police allegedly roughed up German demonstrators at Moravská Ostrava, to break off the talks.[17]

Sensing the growing possibility of war, that same day France called up its reserves. Several days earlier, Great Britain had sent out its fleet. Both countries explained their actions as routine maneuvers, but in its editorial "Mobilization Is Not War," the *New York Times* rejected the French and British denials concerning their preparations for war. Accordingly, it declared that Europe was becoming an armed camp. As for the Czechoslovak concessions, the newspaper predicted that the country would become a Nazi puppet state, but hoped that "Perhaps this is the best guarantee that the decision will not be for war." It added this caveat: the decision rested with unpredictable Hitler, who, the paper correctly claimed, had been directing Sudeten policy.[18]

Other sources commented on the negotiations in similar fashion. The *Baltimore Sun* expressed amazement at the stalled negotiations since the Czechoslovak concessions would have been unthinkable a short time ago. Yet, the Sudeten demands of autonomy for all Germans in Czechoslovakia remained ridiculous. Echoing the sentiment expressed earlier in the *Honolulu Advertiser*, it announced that the demands "are impossible no matter how approached. As well expect the United States to give autonomy to Germans scattered through the Yorkville neighborhood of New York [C]ity."[19] *Life* applauded Beneš for his "brilliant game of civics, pulling forms of government out of his hat like a conjurer."[20] The *Wall Street Journal* saw through the Sudeten thinly veiled excuse for ending negotiations, and viewed Beneš's actions as a genuine attempt at resolution. Instead, an "obscure incident in a border village," described as a "tupenny brawl," contrived by "Chancellor Hitler's marionettes" ended this possibility. Thus these events proved the uselessness of trying to predict the future. What mattered was the position of Germany, not the affected parties in Czechoslovakia. The paper further wondered about Germany's final stance at the Nuremberg meeting since the threat of war had caused American business activity to stagnate. The financial paper concluded, "The world can only continue to watch Hitler continue to throw rocks near the window—trying to see how close he can come without breaking it."[21] Howard Brubaker also mentioned the negotiations in his weekly *New Yorker* column "Of All Things." This satirist and short story writer was known for concise and humorous paragraphs often infusing world affairs with American events. He compared Beneš's troubles in dealings with the Czechoslovak Germans with that of President Franklin D. Roosevelt's current difficult attempts to purge conservative Democrats who opposed many of his New Deal programs.[22]

No one could be sure of Hitler's next step in the deepening crisis. In its editorial "Nearing Zero Hour," the *Baltimore Sun* echoed the *Wall Street Journal* and *New York Times* by stating that the decision for war no longer rested with Czechoslovakia or the Sudeten Germans, but with Hitler.[23] The *New Orleans Times-Picayune*, in its editorial

"Watchfully Waiting," agreed that Hitler was the key to war.[24] The Los Angeles paper concurred with its Baltimore and New Orleans counterparts in its commentary "Will It Be War?" Again referring to Hitler's imminent speech to his party's congress, the daily anxiously opined, "All the world can do now is to wait and hope sanity will prevail."[25] Under such tense circumstances, the *New York Times* applauded French Premier Edouard Daladier's move in ending a dock strike in Marseilles, and repealing the forty-hour work week as means of readying his country for the possibility of war.[26] *Life*, however, took a different view of the French leader's action, seeing it not as a sign of strength but one in which the war situation so frightened Daladier that he canceled the forty hour week. But to show how tough the French premier could be, the photo journal published a full page photograph of the usually dour Daladier confidently smiling while sitting behind his desk in the war ministry under a Gobelin tapestry depicting the victorious French King Louis XIV at the Battle of Dôle.[27]

The British succeeded in restarting the stalled talks on September 9. The *New York Times* believed the British had pursued such a policy to prevent a repetition of the events in late July and early August 1914, when the European powers parleyed very little before the outbreak of war. The tone of the editorial remained pessimistic by noting that uncertainty had increased when such negotiations "are turned on and off like water in a spigot." Like earlier editorials in the *Baltimore Sun, New Orleans Times-Picayune, Los Angeles Times,* and *Wall Street Journal,* the New York daily again emphasized that real decisions were made elsewhere, namely Germany.[28] The newspaper continued along this theme the next day. History proved that major powers could use any pretext for starting a war. For example, the assassination of the Austro-Hungarian heir apparent in Sarajevo, in 1914, sparked the First World War and the Marco Polo Bridge Incident where the Japanese provoked an intentional clash with the Chinese in 1937, thereby touching off the Asian phase of the Second World War. Hence, the issue of Czechoslovakia really did not matter. Rather, foreseeing the events of the coming weeks, the *New York Times* predicted that the possible outbreak of war would be decided by how far Germany could proceed without provoking the British.[29]

Newspapers sometimes contradicted themselves in the same issue. Interestingly, on the same page, the *New York Times* featured its regular op-ed "Europe" by Anne O'Hare McCormick that featured a different opinion of the situation. In her work subtitled "Factors Stronger Than Hitler Will Decide Peace or War," McCormick remarked that Hitler had no reliable allies while a greater coalition, including the Soviet Union, pledged to fight with France against him. She mistakenly reasoned, "Be sure that the decisive word will not be spoken in Germany."[30] The New Orleans daily disagreed with McCormick's assessment. Although Czechoslovakia had allies, the refusal of Great Britain to join the other two European powers increased the risk of war. The newspaper scolded England for "playing thus with the hands of the rapid Nazis." Still, it predicted that Great Britain would be forced to oppose Germany if war erupted.[31]

As the crisis intensified, speeches by the American envoys to Paris and London, which did not take into account the strength of American isolationism at home, forced President Roosevelt to take a stand to distance himself from these remarks. In early September, William C. Bullitt, ambassador to France, speaking in Bordeaux, reportedly stated that the United States and France were "indefectively united in war as in peace." At the same time, Joseph P. Kennedy, ambassador to Great Britain, publicly attacked "certain countries" that denied the freedom of religious worship. Europeans interpreted both addresses to signify that America sided with the two West European democracies.[32] The *New York Times* echoed European sentiment, inferring American involvement in the crisis by stating: "In any real test of strength, provoked by German aggression, she (Germany) can count on the certain hostility of every democratic nation."[33] *Time* claimed the envoys' discourses pressured Hitler,[34] while the *New Republic* praised the ambassadors, seeing their speeches presumably with Roosevelt's blessing, as the first American move away from its isolationism toward an active role in world affairs.[35] The *Chicago Tribune* agreed, maintaining that Bullitt's remarks had paved the way for Roosevelt to enter a European war. The newspaper's owner, Colonel Robert R. McCormick, advocated rapid isolationist and anti-Roosevelt stances. He viewed almost every action of the president as leading the country to socialism. As a result, the paper forecasted that this American involvement would be the first step that would lead the country to a communist dictatorship.[36] It appeared that McCormick believed that if the United States became involved in another European war it would end up much like Imperial Russia in 1917, with the overthrow of the government and the triumph of Bolshevism.

Roosevelt, mindful of isolationist strength, quickly distanced himself from his ambassadors' remarks by blaming journalists for misinterpreting not only these speeches, but others by himself and the Secretary of State Cordell Hull. At a press conference on September 9, the president asserted that journalists were "100 % wrong" in their assessments,[37] and the media was "trying to create a war scare." *Newsweek* expressed dissatisfaction with the president's remarks and chastised him for inaction: "Last week's events put the Roosevelt-Hull Foreign Policy right back where it has been for five years—shutting between isolationism and intervention.... It thereby serves notice on those trying to shove the United States toward a foreign conflict ... that no one can presume in advance where America will stand."[38]

The Nazi Party Congress

While negotiations resumed between the Czechoslovaks and the Sudeten Germans, both Beneš and German Field Marshal Herman Göring took to the airwaves on September 10. Beneš explained his government's actions, and urged ethnic harmony, reason, and calm in Czechoslovakia. He ended his address to his countrymen by stating, "Let us be ready to make sacrifices but let us be optimists even in a time of great difficulties. Above all, let us not forget that faith will move mountains and that they will bring us happily out of all present European situations." In contrast, during part of his two hour unrestrained speech to the Nazi Party Congress, Göring verbally attacked Czechoslovakia. He ranted: "I do not deny there is a crisis. A small section of Europe is pestering minorities and has caused international unrest.... But we know what is going on. That little chit of a race devoid of culture is oppressing a civilized minority and behind all this is Moscow and the eternal Jewish devil's grimace."[39]

The American press reacted favorably to Beneš's effort to preserve the peace. The *New York Times* characterized Beneš's speech as a "measured, pacific, statesmanlike plea,"[40] while *Time* called it "a calm, firm and tactful broadcast" in an effort to calm the people of Czechoslovakia. It noted that the editor of the *New York Post* "praised the speech" as "'a model of what a public utterance should be,'" and, on the same page, published a photograph of a stoic Beneš sitting behind a microphone.[41] The *Baltimore Sun* also lauded the Czechoslovak president's remarks: "His were words of a man not merely anxious to avert war but anxious to make a strong showing for history,"[42] while

Newsweek claimed, "Beneš has built a reputation for the iciest set of nerves in Europe."[43] In its next issue the *Baltimore Sun* continued to approve of Beneš in an editorial "Fine Example." Although bullied by Germany, the Czechoslovaks retained their wits, and proved an example to be emulated: "The Czechs, despite the strain they have felt and still feel, the anger they have known and must still know, have given a splendid demonstration of how democracy works and of how fit they are to conduct their own affairs and given time and good will, to solve their country's problems."[44]

In contrast, some American papers and magazines took a dim view of Göring's speech. For example, the Baltimore daily pointed out that Göring's actions showed which side was the instigator in the crisis.[45] The *New Yorker's* Brubaker wryly remarked that the field marshal's characterization of Czechs as uncultured Jews unwilling to commit suicide was a "terrific indictment."[46] *Time* claimed Göring's "exhausting fury" so harmed his health that doctors ordered him back to Berlin to recover away from the tumult of the congress. Rather than assess the field marshal's radio address, the weekly magazine included a quote from the *London Times* describing it as a "'speech of a bully whose fury makes even sympathizers with the German case forget whatever there is in that case for legitimate sympathy.'"[47]

Despite such sentiments, Göring's and Beneš's speeches remained inconsequential as the world waited for the Führer's address closing the party congress on September 12. The *New Orleans Times-Picayune* noted that Göring and other high ranking Nazis had set the congress tempo for Hitler's speech in which war or peace would be decided: "Under the influence of the tom-tom beating and war dancing the fuehrer was hailed as 'divinely inspired' and infallible."[48] *Life* described Hitler's demands to this point as "laughable" and "shadow boxing," but speculated that the German leader hoped his actions would force the Czechoslovaks to capitulate to grant him a "smash finale" for the end of the congress.[49]

Although Hitler verbally assailed Czechoslovakia, he remained restrained and only demanded self-determination for the Sudeten Germans. This, as *Life* reported, incited them to further violence.[50] Thus, as the *Chicago Tribune, Los Angeles Times*, and *New Orleans Times-Picayune* noted, Hitler's speech did nothing to resolve the crisis but only added to the suspense.[51] The *Honolulu Advertiser, New York Times*, and *Baltimore Sun* agreed. Moreover, the newspapers expressed gratitude that his speech did not result in war but in another day of peace.[52] The Los Angeles daily believed one could read anything into his address, but at "face value," it had an encouraging tone. The problem remained that Hitler could not be taken at "face value."[53] Still, despite its subdued tone, the *New York Times* characterized Hitler's speech as an ultimatum much like that which Austria-Hungary issued to Serbia in 1914. The Czechoslovaks would be forced to fight as did the Serbs. Such action resulted in a world war that ultimately doomed Austria-Hungary, the paper wrote, thus implying that Germany, too, would eventually lose.[54] In a two-page spread, *Life* quoted and illustrated the key sections of the Führer's three hour speech describing it as "full of superficial, simplified history of events." To give credence to this remark, the photo journal noted that the Sudeten Germans were citizens of Austria-Hungary prior to World War One and not Germany. It thus concluded that "Hitler's claim to them is geographically fantastic."[55]

Articles in the small town *Salisbury Times, Newsweek,* and the *New Yorker* offered mixed reactions to Hitler's speech. The Salisbury newspaper also noted that Hitler's oration did nothing to solve Germany's problems with Czechoslovakia, but believed that as the days passed the possibility of war lessened.[56] In contrast, *Newsweek* believed that the crisis was the most dangerous since the First World War.[57] *New Yorker's* Brubaker noted that the crisis brought the planet to "an unprecedented state of jitters. Peace and civilization" rested with Hitler "who," the satirist noted, "has a strong prejudice against both of them."[58] The *Salisbury Times* warned, however, that Germany would eventually go to war over the Sudeten issue. But, for the paper, peace was worth sacrificing Czechoslovakia: "A hard bargain is being driven with Czechoslovakia, playing the role of sucker, but from a diplomatic point of view postponing a war is worth that price."[59]

The Crisis Continues

As the crisis deepened with unrest and fighting between the Sudeten Germans and Czechs breaking out in border regions of Czechoslovakia, the Czechoslovak government proclaimed martial law in some areas of the Sudetenland. It appeared that Germany would use the violence as a pretext to invade Czechoslovakia. The New Orleans daily noted that the Nazi press "magnified" every incident, many of which seemed to be planned in Germany, thereby increasing the threat of war. It remained ironic, the paper stated, that Czechoslovakia imposed martial law to restore order while the Sudetens and Nazis assailed Prague's inability to control the situation, and demanded the order be revoked.[60] The *Los Angeles Times* approved of Czechoslovakia's imposition of martial law. Not only was it in the interest of all citizens of the Sudetenland, its continuance was vital to preserve the country's sovereignty.[61]

Such developments did not sit well with American financial markets. The *Wall Street Journal* fretted that the flight of European capital based on the strong prospect of war had caused the American security market to drop precipitously over the past several days. It feared a European conflict could have an adverse affect on businesses since the belligerents would not import nonessential goods from the United States. Furthermore, it blamed Roosevelt for the Neutrality Acts which could adversely damage war-related commerce. Accordingly, it reacted negatively toward total American neutrality by concluding, "We do not yet know whether we are willing to pay the price of abstention from all war trade."[62] Indeed, the *Wall Street Journal* proved correct in its assessment. Isolationism, a backlash against American involvement in the First World War, inspired the 1930s neutrality legislation as a means to prevent the United States from becoming entangled in another foreign war. Such laws established a prohibition on the exportation to belligerents of many items including weapons, war material, and the granting of loans and credits.[63]

Four days later on September 19, the *Wall Street Journal* changed this position. In its editorial "Keeping Out of War," it now foresaw that the neutrality laws would be "negligible" particularly on the shipments of munitions. This situation, the paper warned, would repeat the same scenario from the First World War precisely that which the Neutrality Acts were designed to avoid. Although the supplying of belligerents would occur, it would be one sided like World War One. In a conflict between Great Britain, France, and Germany, the British and French navies would permit these countries to purchase and import just about anything while effectively stopping German overseas trade. In another example, in a conflict between Germany and Japan versus Czechoslovakia and the Soviet Union, the Germans and Japanese with their superior navies would have the economic advantage. As a result, the deprived sides of Germany in the first case and the USSR and Czechoslovakia in the second would not view their overseas trade positions objectively but would search for scapegoats. Such situations could potentially harm American neutrality since the United States would definitely be seen as favoring one side over the other. This occurred when Americans granted loans and goods to the Allies rather than to the Central Powers of Germany and Austria-Hungary over twenty years ago during the First World War thereby causing Germany to resort to unrestricted submarine warfare bringing the United States into the war. The paper warned that the "wooden" neutrality legislation maintained peace on very shaky grounds. Rather than laws, the financial giant believed the will of the people, desiring peace expressed through their government, would prevent American involvement in war except in cases of national emergencies.[64]

In an attempt to avert war, British Prime Minister Neville Chamberlain flew to Germany to meet with Hitler at Berchtesgaden to discuss the issue on September 15. The *Chicago Tribune* viewed the prime minister's trip as a face saving opportunity for Hitler to extricate himself from the situation without a loss of prestige.[65] The *New York Times, Baltimore Sun, New Orleans Times-Picayune, Honolulu Advertiser,* and *Life* all described Chamberlain's action as unprecedented in a final effort to avoid war.[66] *Time* stated that Chamberlain "won the gratitude of most of the world" by flying to Germany.[67] The New York, Baltimore, New Orleans, and Honolulu dailies mentioned the initial results of the discussions remained unknown, keeping the world on the edge of its seat speculating on the content of them.[68]

The *New York Times, Baltimore Sun,* and *Honolulu Advertiser* wondered whether Chamberlain would abandon the Czechoslovaks for peace.[69] If so, the New York and Baltimore papers asked, would the Czechoslovaks fight?[70] Yet, the *New Orleans Times-Picayune*, in its editorial "Chamberlain's Diversion," described the visit as another in a series of unsuccessful British attempts at "appeasement" which it condemned as a policy of "retreats and concessions." All British actions have proved "futile" and "none ... has insured peace nor checked the rather headlong tendency toward conflict." The southern daily remained pessimistic. Even if for some reason an agreement had been reached at Berchtesgaden, it would not mean a lasting peace since modern day treaties were broken at will. The next day, September 17, the same newspaper continued its attack against British appeasement. England's hesitation to support another democracy only increased the "appetite" of the Nazis who interpreted Chamberlain's journey as a "willingness to give them whatever they ask in Central Europe, if only they will refrain awhile from actual war." In contrast to this dishonorable British action, the paper applauded the Czechoslovak acts of martial law and disbanding the Sudeten German party. It concluded, "The sanity and steady courage of the Prague government shines by contrast with the vague and shuffling courses in other European quarters."[71]

For many Americans the cause of the crisis remained unclear. In her semi-monthly *New Yorker* piece entitled, "Letter from Paris," Janet Flanner traveled to East Central Europe where she attempted to make sense of the crisis for her readers. Since 1925, this American expatriate writer and correspondent adroitly detected changing nuances and moods in politics, culture, and the lives of the people about which she wrote under the pseudonym "Genêt." After traveling to East Central Europe in mid-September, Flanner attempted to explain the Czechoslovak-German problem in her article entitled "Letter from Budapest," by referring to the defunct Habsburg empire. Using as a model the former Hungarian territory of Slovakia, containing a large Hungarian population incorporated into Czechoslovakia after World War One, she tried to put the ethnic problem into perspective. Flanner wrote that in the manor houses lived financially strapped Hungarian aristocrats who employed Slovaks as servants, Hungarians as stable hands, Germans as gamekeepers, and Jews as farmers while buying merchandise from Czech businessmen. These various nationalities, at some time in history, controlled the others who have neither forgotten nor forgiven this fact. This ethnic mixing caused difficulties in East Central Europe since none of these nationalities had strong champions outside of their countries. At best, the situation was comical, complicated, and incomprehensible. Yet, there was one major difference with the present circumstances. Flanner correctly noted: "The problem's only novelty consists in the fact that of all these groups, who as underdogs desire the complete autonomy which as top dogs they have always refused to give, only one, the Sudetens, have a Herr Hitler behind them. One suffices." Lastly, gauging the fatalistic mood of the Hungarians during her visit, Flanner wrote that if Germany came to blows with Czechoslovakia, it was widely believed that Hitler would not stop until he swallowed all of East Central Europe.[72]

In such a supercharged European atmosphere some believed that the Czechoslovaks would resist Hitler. *Life* was certain the Czechoslovaks would fight. In its two-page photographic spread on the Czechoslovak military, it included a symbolic picture of two soldiers manning a machine gun, one Czech the other Sudeten German. It boasted that they could not be equated to the Austrians, Chinese, Ethiopians, or Spanish Loyalists who had either capitulated without a fight or experienced defeat in their conflicts. The Czechoslovaks had one of the best armies in Europe, and compared to the other Slavic peoples, they were industrious and have contributed numerous people of note to the world. The photo journal claimed that every Czechoslovak would fight to the death rather than surrender: "Certainly he will use the expensive and effective army he built up and use it with courage, brains and desperation.... They are not frightened by Hitler's titanic threats."[73]

After Chamberlain's return from Germany, the British and French governments conferred. On the following day, Sunday, September 18, the *New York Times* asked all houses of worship to pray for peace in East Central Europe.[74] That same day, Great Britain and France called for the cession of the Sudetenland to Germany, agreeing to arrange a European guarantee of the remainder of Czechoslovakia. Meanwhile, Sudeten volunteer para-military *Freikorps* attacked border installations causing the Czechoslovak government to declare a state of emergency.[75]

The *Baltimore Sun*, the *New Orleans Times-Picayune*, the *Los Angeles Times,* and the *New Republic* were highly critical of the abandonment of Czechoslovakia by the Western democracies. The *Baltimore Sun*'s headlines screamed: "BRITAIN AND FRANCE GIVE IN." In its editorial, written before the news of the desertion of Czechoslovakia, the newspaper commented and speculated on the London discussions. If the French and British sacrificed Czechoslovakia for peace, then they were no better than the Nazis who would now control and direct French and English foreign policies. While warning that Hitler would not be satisfied with such a victory, it negatively characterized the meeting of the two Western governments as "the last stand, perhaps of peace, perhaps of European democracy."[76] The following day, the Baltimore daily conceded that the partitions of Poland by Austria, Prussia, and Russia in the eighteenth century acted as a precedent for the German demands,[77] but maintained that the democracies had destroyed one of their own "bulwarks" in East Central Europe. Rather than mediators in this dispute, it characterized the British and French as "accessories," who made the Czechoslovaks out to be the guilty party with their treatment of the Sudeten Germans.[78] In its editorial "Capitulation," the *New Orleans Times-Picayune* declared that the civilized world was "appalled" by British and French actions since they would neither preserve the peace nor end German demands. Two days later, on September 22, the same paper added that peace may have been temporarily saved, but the New Orleans daily scolded the British and the French by declaring that "war averted by honorable means in the spirit of give and take must be differentiated from an unstable peace gained through submission to force and the wanton sacrifice of principle."[79]

Like its New Orleans complement, the Los Angeles daily viewed Britain's and France's abandonment of Czechoslovakia as a "blunder," which would negatively affect democracy in Europe. By giving in to Hitler, the Western democracies had not preserved the peace, but only postponed war. It considered the proposed guarantee of a rump Czechoslovakia laughable since the Western allies were not willing to guarantee Czechoslovakia's present borders. The newspaper urged "weak kneed" England and France to call Hitler's war bluff, concluding, "There probably will never be a better chance to do it than now." When the two countries did not take a stand against Germany, three days later, on September 21, the same paper expressed its disgust with England and France by observing that they had "been buffaloed by the bully of Berlin. It is a strange site."[80] The *New Republic* also published a scathing article about the democracies' action entitled, "The Great Surrender," stating, "The decision ... to sacrifice Czechoslovakia to the Nazi Moloch seems like the ultimate in cowardice and faithlessness, which it is impossible to justify while retaining a shred of self-respect or trust in the supposed integrity of democracy." The magazine noted that the United States had much to learn from the mistakes of the European events such as keeping promises and an unwavering foreign policy.[81]

In contrast to this biting, negative assessment of the Western allies' appeasement, several papers promoted an American isolationist stance in response to the apparent outcome of the crisis. A *Honolulu Advertiser* editorial stated, "In solemn conversations French and British leaders have reached the practical decision that it is better to avoid a serious war than to attempt to save an infant republic that has never been much more than an experiment. So far as the good of the world is concerned this is a wise decision."[82] The *Salisbury Times* agreed with this assessment, and continued along this venue the next day believing that although democracy was in crisis abroad, the United States would make a grave mistake by intervening.[83] The *New York Times* offered a poignant observation that Americans might question the judgment of the Western democracies, but could not criticize their actions. The United States played a major role in the creation of Czechoslovakia during the First World War, but after its establishment America refused to help it in any manner. Subsequently, the United States had no cause to urge the horrors and dangers of war on others while it did not assume its global responsibilities.[84] The Los Angeles daily disagreed with its New York counterpart although it concurred that the United States had practically created the country. As such, the honorable thing for America to do was to oppose the dismemberment of Czechoslovakia. Noting the difficulty of this measure due to isolationism, it timidly wrote: "It is not clear, however, that any stand we might take would even influence the situation, much less be decisive." Quickly forgetting American honor in favor of an isolationist sentiment, it concluded since Great Britain and France had abandoned Czechoslovakia, "We have at least ample precedent for keeping entirely out of the quarrel."[85]

The *Wall Street Journal* also expressed an isolationist position in the second part of its editorial entitled "Keeping out of War." In the current crisis, one could easily assign blame but when the horrors of war appear, it would quickly bring one back to reality: "The mere thought of the United States participating in the holocaust is repugnant to us." As such, it was not difficult to understand the stance of the Western democracies: "What would it be if we were seriously challenged to 'put up or shut up' in regard to a foreign nation to which we *had* made commitments?" The United States would be in the same situation as the Western allies which may have lost prestige due to their unfulfilled promises to Czechoslovakia. Despite this loss, times have changed since Britain and France made these assurances which the newspaper claimed their people never really supported. Attempts by Great Britain and France to persuade President Roosevelt to take a leadership role in the crisis failed as Americans remained unwilling to resort to force. Although the *Wall Street Journal* expressed hope that war could be avoided, it applauded America's "aloofness" during the recent events calling it a "wise" decision: "President Roosevelt and Secretary Hull will doubtless continue in the path they have so sanely chosen during the past weeks of tension."[86]

On September 20, Prague called for negotiations with Berlin on the basis of the 1925 Locarno Treaty in which Germany agreed to arbitrate disputes with Czechoslovakia and other countries that had signed the arrangement. Whereas the *New York Times* viewed this move by Prague as a delaying tactic,[87] the *Baltimore Sun* applauded it as "astute" because it showed that Czechoslovakia retained its sovereignty and wanted to negotiate on the same level as those nations which have been deciding its fate up to this point. It hoped these requested talks would gain time for cooler heads to prevail.[88]

The possible application of the Locarno treaty to defuse the crisis led the New Orleans daily to note that its current events contest for Louisiana and Mississippi high schoolers would shortly begin. Ironically, the paper stated the contest had started in 1925 when the possibility of war lessened due to the treaties resulting from the meeting at Locarno and the earlier Washington Conference, the latter having promoted naval disarmament. Thirteen years later there would be no shortage of material for the contestants as the 1925 agreements had neither prevented crises nor decreased the possibility of war. With the problems in East Central Europe, the *New Orleans Times-Picayune* predicted that students would have plenty to write about "in the rearing again of that debased doctrine that might makes right; in the rumblings that may well augur a turning point in civilization not easily comprehensible."[89]

London and Paris rejected Prague's move to preserve the peace through Locarno and demanded that the German conditions be accepted. Cognizant of its isolation, Czechoslovakia agreed to the wishes of the Western democracies on September 21. The *Chicago Tribune* stated that the leaders of Czechoslovakia knew there was no alternative in the face of overwhelming odds, and hoped that history would grant them a special place for their brave decision not to resort to war.[90] The *New York Times* expressed relief that the founder of the republic, Thomas G. Masaryk, had died the year before, and would not see his creation partitioned, while sadly, Beneš, who worked with Masaryk for the establishment of the state, would witness this tragedy.[91] *Newsweek* explained that Great Britain and France abandoned Czechoslovakia when they realized that their populations would not fight for it.[92] The *Los Angeles Times* believed that Czecho-slovakia gave in not due to pressure from Hitler, but to Great Britain and France which "have sold their stepchild down the river and got a brick of gold." By doing so, the Western allies have given Hitler "the key to Europe." In concluding its editorial, "No Bargain," the paper reiterated its previous comments that England and France should have called Germany's bluff: "From this distance it looks as if the time to have stopped Hitler was four days ago and that the French and British have missed the boat." The next day, September 23, in its commentary, "Its Not All Over, Yet," the same newspaper seemed more optimistic. Although Czechoslovakia had lost its allies and was surrounded by hostile neighbors including Poland and Hungary, like *Life*, the west coast daily claimed that history had shown that one should not prematurely count out its determined people: "The Czechs may go down before overwhelmingly superior force, but they are likely to go down fighting."[93]

Due to the Czechoslovak capitulation, the government of Premier Milan Hodža was replaced by another led by popular General Jan Syrový. *Life* described the event as the "[c]limax of Czechoslovakia's anguish...."[94] The Los Angeles paper commented that the resignation of the Hodža government was a foregone conclusion in light of events. It approved of Beneš's selection of the "able ... national hero" Syrový as the new premier since it gave a stronger message to the Germans by increasing the military presence in the Czechoslovak government. Yet, the daily praised the Czechoslovak president for not installing a military dictatorship in this time of crisis: "Preservation of republican principles is ... a stronger defense than bullets against external aggression and internal dissension."[95]

Meanwhile, Chamberlain returned to Germany to confer with Hitler at Godesberg, where he received more demands including the immediate surrender of the Sudetenland. *New Yorker*'s Brubaker noted sarcastically that the sentimental Hitler chose this location due to an earlier success. Referring to the Nazi purge "Night of the Long Knives," Brubaker wrote that Hitler had "spent many happy hours there in 1934 planning the murder of his Nazi pals."[96] Czechoslovakia, Great Britain, and France, however, rejected the Godesberg ultimatum and prepared for war. The *Los Angeles Times* seemed cheerful at the prospect of war. Czechoslovakia and its allies had called Hitler's bluff. By doing so, the newspaper stated, they had probably saved the peace since Germany could not face an overwhelming coalition. The following day, September 25, the same daily credited Czechoslovakia for the recent turn in events. The isolated country had agreed to the terms when Hitler "overplayed his hand." The Czechoslovaks decided to resist, placing the "one-eyed, fighting wildcat" Syrový as new premier and mobilizing. Stunned, France, backed by Britain and the Soviet Union, agreed to fight causing Hitler to show "the yellow streak that is the hallmark of a bully of whatever race or exalted might." The German leader realized that if war came about his country would lose. This was his first defeat. Noting as it had on several occasions on calling Hitler's bluff, the paper concluded that "The incidents of the past few days have made it plain enough that yielding to a threat of force was a mistake, but if they add anything to the permanence of resulting peace they may be worth their cost."[97]

To Ludwig Lore, an anti-Nazi German immigrant journalist, author, and *New York Post* editorial staff member,[98] war seemed certain. In an article published in the October issue of *Independent Woman*, Lore, who admitted writing the piece late in the late night and early morning of September 25/26 during the height of the crisis, described the situation as white hot. He wondered about Hitler's upcoming speech scheduled for that day. Would he "send millions- the flower of the world's youth—to death and destruction?" When Lore visited Europe during the previous summer, leaders told him another conflict could arise but not before 1939 or 1940 since no country was prepared for war. Yet, Hitler and Mussolini, fooled by the passive responses of the Western democracies to the Italian invasion of Ethiopia in 1935, the Spanish Civil War, and the *Anschluss* turned aggressively toward Czechoslovakia. The socialist Lore stated that the small East Central European country surprised them by resisting, and gained the support of the masses of France and Britain who resented the continued appeasement of their governments. If Hitler backed down, the peoples, not the leaders of the Western allies, deserved the credit for their willingness to resort to war. But, Lore warned, if Hitler took the Sudetenland, it would result in his domination of Central and Eastern Europe and the destruction of the USSR. He wrote that if miraculously war had been adverted by the time subscribers read his article, it would be due, he erroneously noted, to the Western democracies strong, unified response to fascist aggression. He wondered whether the United States would join Great Britain and

France or maintain its isolationism. But if war erupted, he also blamed America for refusing to supply even moral support to the Western democracies during the crisis.[99]

Lore would be bitterly disappointed as events unfolded over the following week. The Germans did not back down. In another speech at the Sports Palast in Berlin on September 26, Hitler proclaimed that his patience had evaporated, and that he would invade Czechoslovakia by October 1, if his demands were not met. War again seemed imminent. As the *New Orleans Times-Picayune* noted, Hitler's speech was hardly conciliatory. It was meant to increase German morale and passion. The following day the same paper commented that if war occurred Hitler would not be the only one to blame. Other nations, especially Great Britain and France, would share this responsibility since they did nothing over the years to stop him because they "do not want to fight except in defense of their own soil."[100] The *Chicago Tribune* believed that the United States had no place in a war for the mastery of Europe. It maintained that "The rest of the world seems intent upon suicide. It is our right and our duty to preserve sanity and civilization here. By keeping ourselves clear of Europe's quarrels we gain the additional advantage of preserving our right to keep Europe from interfering in America."[101]

Other newspapers were more optimistic about the maintenance of peace. The *Honolulu Advertiser* characterized Hitler's address as less bellicose and mild as compared to his earlier speeches, resulting in less tension and greater hope in resolving the crisis.[102] The *Baltimore Sun* agreed stating that his speech was "really open ended," but kept great psychological pressure on the British and French.[103] Both the *New York Times* and *Baltimore Sun* believed that Hitler misjudged the response to Godesberg and might have to back down in face of a larger coalition.[104] Although the Los Angeles daily described the address as might makes right, it agreed with its New York and Baltimore complements. Hitler may have exhausted his patience, but Great Britain, France, and the Soviet Union have also lost theirs with the German leader who has now forgotten his passion for war in face of a greater coalition. The next several days, the paper cautioned, would decide how far Hitler could go in his trek toward European and possible global domination.[105]

The possibility of war unnerved American leaders. *Newsweek* reported that the American government advised its citizens to be ready to leave Europe. The State Department's press secretary unsuccessfully attempted to display calm when discussing the issue by lighting a lit cigarette. Ambassador Kennedy allegedly forecasted war, and urged correspondents to send their families from London as he had, while talking about moving the embassy from soon-to-be bombed London.[106] *Time* related that the American ambassador to Prague had begun converting his wine cellar into a bomb shelter. It also claimed that in an event of war, Washington insiders believed an even chance existed that Roosevelt would attempt to repeal the Neutrality Acts of the 1930s. The magazine predicted that the president, however, would be humiliated in his efforts by moves to pass a constitutional amendment requiring a national referendum for war.[107] Although the government seemed edgy, many Americans felt safe, sound, and isolated from events across the Atlantic Ocean. *New Yorker's* Brubaker mocked this ideal by noting the September 21 hurricane that hit Long Island and New England killing about 600: "While we were thanking God for the Atlantic Ocean, it turned upon us with unbridled fury."[108]

In the early morning of September 26, President Roosevelt issued an appeal to Beneš and Hitler for further negotiations to resolve the problem and to avoid world war. To some, this implied American involvement. The *Baltimore Sun* approved of Roosevelt's statement and viewed it as proof the administration sided with the Western powers and intended to take an active role in global affairs much to the chagrin of isolationists.[109] The *New York Times* hoped that Germany would heed the president's appeal, and if not, then to the whole world it would remain the aggressor.[110] In his piece "Of All That," the *New Yorker's* Brubaker believed that all Americans across the mainstream political spectrum supported the president's initiatives by noting that former president Herbert Hoover told a Republican rally in Kansas City, "The president will find every Republican and every thinking person behind him in that effort." Thereby, for Brubaker, "Making it unanimous" that all Americans supported the president's peace efforts.[111]

Other papers and periodicals reacted less favorable to Roosevelt's proposal. The *New Republic* saw Roosevelt's action as an empty gesture,[112] while *Newsweek* characterized the president's move as influenced by rising popular American sympathy for Czechoslovakia that granted unsubstantiated support to Great Britain and France without any intention of commitment.[113] The isolationist *Chicago Tribune* believed that his appeal might have been effective if the United States had actually been neutral. Instead, the paper insisted that Roosevelt had already aligned the country against Germany and his note constituted a first step that would lead the United States toward involvement in a European war. In its concluding paragraph, the newspaper urged that "We maintain our sanity and resist the communist-inspired effort to engage us in the conflict."[114] This appeal hardly expressed the leadership the world had hoped the president would assume as indicated the previous week in the *Wall Street Journal.* The paper described the plea as a "justifiable effort to avert a calamity," but wondered if it would have any effect since it contained no indication of any American commitment. It hoped that the appeal would bring the potential belligerents back to their senses when they realized the full implications of war and resolve the Sudeten issue peaceably so world economic recovery could continue with the United States leading the way.[115]

The deepening crisis and grave possibility of war could be seen even beyond the reporting of the news and editorials. In the philatelic section of the Sunday, September 25 issue of the *New York Times,* an article contemplated whether announced Czechoslovak stamps slated for October would be released or if Germany would issue a commemorative for its acquisition of the Sudetenland. It predicted that if Czechoslovakia ceased to exist, collectors would send prices soaring for some of its stamps.[116]

The Munich Agreement

On September 28, in one last attempt to avert war, Chamberlain announced to parliament a proposed four-power summit of Great Britain, France, Italy, and Germany to which Hitler agreed. Neither Czechoslovakia nor its and France's ally the Soviet Union were invited to the conference. The print media held its breath and welcomed news of the talks. The cautiously hopeful *Honolulu Advertiser, Baltimore Sun, Los Angeles Times,* and *New York Times* respectively entitled their editorials concerning the upcoming discussions "War Clouds Lift," "Hope Revived," "Back from the Brink," and "Respite from War."[117] The *Chicago Tribune* likewise expressed optimism that the talks might preserve peace.[118]

The *Wall Street Journal* took a more reserved stance. Its editorial "The Turning Point?" erroneously believed that Hitler had proposed the talks. Furthermore, it mentioned that world public opinion for peace pressured the leaders to the negotiations, but it would remain for the historians to assign the real credit. By going to Munich, Chamberlain once again appealed to mankind's conscience as he did when he traveled to Berchtesgaden and Godesberg earlier in the month. Many people saw these journeys as an affront to British prestige, but if the summit averted war then this loss of prestige would be meaningless compared to the horrors of a conflict. The financial newspaper also expressed its belief that Roosevelt's plea of September 26, in which he appealed for reason, had played a role in bringing the leaders together at Munich. Expressing isolationist sentiment, it noted that although Americans would continue not to commit themselves abroad, "we do not and cannot detach ourselves from the human race; we do not imagine ourselves indifferent to what may happen to its standards of civilization." It concluded by stating the world anticipated much from Munich, but that it should not expect speedy remedies to Europe's many problems caused by the First World War and its resulting "unhappy" peace treaties. The process would take time, but hopefully, during the next twenty-four hours, Munich would show that peaceful resolutions remained possible.[119]

The *New Yorker*, on the other hand, chided the British government for retaining antiquated and meaningless traditions. Chamberlain wasted precious time by conferring with a powerless monarch when immediate action was needed. It lamented, "No people but the British … would have taken time out for this little excursion with fantasy. The Prime Minister goes to ask the opinion of a bewildered young man whom nobody expects to have one and to whom nobody would pay the slightest attention if he had."[120]

During the next two days, the leaders of France, Germany, Great Britain, and Italy decided the fate of Czechoslovakia at Munich. According to the provisions of the agreement signed on September 29, Czechoslovakia would evacuate and surrender the Sudetenland to Germany under conditions established by an international commission, and it would receive a British and France guarantee of its new borders. President Roosevelt and Secretary of State Cordell Hull publicly expressed relief that the crisis had ended, but said no more with regard to the conference and the pact.[121] *Newsweek* read into these remarks that the administration believed that the settlement had "victimized" Czechoslovakia and would not bring about permanent peace.[122]

The majority of the sources examined here appreciated the preservation of peace but recognized that it would be difficult to maintain. *Newsweek* laconically noted, "The Munich conference wiped out the war danger in eight hours."[123] The *New York Times* began its editorial "The Price Of Peace," by stating "Let no man say that too high a price has been paid for peace in Europe until he has searched his soul and found himself willing to risk in war the lives of those who are nearest and dearest to him." The tone of the editorial soon changed by noting failed collective security paid this price for peace. It ended with the hope that all nations, including the United States, would rally in an attempt to revive collective security to enforce the peace in the future. Unfortunately, until then, it predicted war and violence would continue to reign globally. In another editorial on the same day, September 30, the *New York Times* gave a summary of the crisis that led to the pact concluding that "[f]rom first to last in the recital of the most dramatic and perhaps most fateful chapters in modern history it is clear that there was no attempt to save anything but the peace." But the paper remained skeptical of the prospects for peace by concluding that "The sequel will show whether the effort was justified."[124]

The *Chicago Tribune,* in an editorial entitled, "A Peace Or A Truce," viewed the agreement along the same vein, declaring that peace had been saved for the moment. The key to the maintenance of this peace remained Hitler. If he made no more demands then it would be permanent, if not, then Munich was a mere pause. The following day, on October 1, the paper noted that Hitler received everything he asked for in the agreement thereby restoring to Germany the influence and honor it had lost with the Treaty of Versailles. As a result, it expected European tensions to calm. However, due to Europe's numerous nationalities and the strange division of the continent into numerous small uneconomically feasible countries, problems remained. The Chicago daily expressed confidence that these difficulties would not cause war for a least a generation. For the paper, this relaxation of tensions meant the United States could resume its isolationism unimpeded. Still it could not resist chiding Roosevelt and Hull for their actions abroad including East Central Europe:

> Under pressure from national groups in this country more especially to acquire personal importance and social prestige, men concerned with our foreign relations have shown a woeful

indifference to America's welfare. They have been busily pulling chestnuts out of the fire for other nations regardless of the risk to America. It is hoped that this kind of toadyism, which is at once repulsive and dangerous will now cease.[125]

The *Honolulu Advertiser* praised the agreement by writing, "The strong powers undoubtedly chose the wisest course in averting war." Whereas history would venerate Chamberlain for his actions in keeping the peace, the territorial paper's commentary continued by strangely noting that Roosevelt and the United States would receive credit for their positive role in the crisis. Like the *New York Times*, it ended on a guarded note: "But the real test is yet to come."[126]

The *New Orleans Times-Picayune* also seemed relieved that war had been averted. It called reports from Munich "encouraging," and that the summit showed "there is some reason and perhaps a little humanity still astray in Europe, and that holocaustic war is not to be fought." Yet the daily continued to chastise Great Britain and France since the agreement could not "change the essential fact that an ally had been deserted and the democratic front shattered." It concluded its editorial on a hopeful note that dishonorable appeasement would not continue: "The dynamite that tears the just and the unjust remains unexploded, still at the hand of any who may believe that murder and suicide are preferable to anything that thwarts aggrandizement."[127]

The *Los Angeles Times* remained cautiously optimistic, although the euphoria accompanying the pact caused people to accept readily the notion that the arrangement had secured long term peace. Despite this, in view of the alternative of war, the paper hailed the agreement: "It rates among the first diplomatic achievements of history." It continued by noting that if the agreement was carried out honestly, benefits could be achieved, but, "'if' is still a big one," since Hitler's promises were hard to believe. Would Czechoslovakia accept the agreement was another "if." But, the west coast daily snidely concluded, "In truth, she (Czechoslovakia) has little choice in the matter."[128]

Life, too, seemed optimistic after characterizing the week's events that culminated in the agreement as "the tensest ... since 1918," and the conference as the "modern world's greatest meeting of Number Ones." To the editors of this magazine, the partition of Czechoslovakia was nothing more than traditional great power diplomacy in action. Indeed, the weekly magazine saw the pact as a setback for

Hitler since he had to accept his demands in a peaceful and legal manner, and the talks brought Germany back to the ideals of "collective bargaining" where democratic discussion rather than bullying triumphed. Finally, it predicted a bright future for Germany if it kept its word, and when the day arrived to erect a statue of Chamberlain, the form would be based upon the prime minister descending from an airplane to symbolize his unprecedented three trips to keep the peace.[129]

In its editorial, "The Great War Ends," the *Wall Street Journal* placed a rather odd interpretation of Munich. It noted that in late 1917, American General Tasker Howard Bliss predicted the First World War would last thirty years. The general believed the battles would end within two years, but the war itself would continue in other ways while the belligerents rebuilt their strength. The armistice of 1918 only halted, but did not end the war. Many people misjudged the Treaties of Versailles and Trianon, thinking they had concluded the war, but their terms could not end the conflict. Instead, they generated more problems that rendered the treaties, bit by bit, useless thus bringing Europe to the brink of another armed conflict "which promised to wipe out what was still left of Western civilization." The paper opined that the Munich Agreement finally brought closure to the First World War after twenty-four years. The desire for peace, as shown at Munich, hopefully would continue to spread thereby ending the Spanish Civil War and Japanese aggression in Asia. It concluded with a thoughtful paragraph influenced by the idea that World War One was the war to end all wars: "It is hardly thinkable that the present generation of men who have with unanimous undisguised and unrestrained joy welcomed this gleam of peace can be induced by any consideration whatever again to turn their backs upon it and take up arms against each other."[130]

Back from Budapest, Janet Flanner in her October 2 "Letter from Paris," described for the American public the situation in France during the height of the crisis. The normally excitable French mobilized their forces, but made no elaborate plans for civilians in case of air raids. Gasoline was hoarded, refugees streamed into Paris, and the American embassy prepared to evacuate its citizens. People remained glued to their radios for British, German, Russian, French, and Czechoslovak news reports. During the evening of Thursday, September 29, Flanner noted wryly that the Sudeten Germans and Czechoslovaks broadcasted horror stories about the other in English with Southern and Brooklyn accents respectively. Europe held its breath until about 10:30 pm when the agreement was announced. Flanner stated, "It was the perfect bedtime story. France slept that night for the first time in a week." For his efforts, French Premier Daladier received an enthusiastic homecoming. Although mobilization cost France, and caused the value of the franc to drop, peace was worth it. The only continued signs of war in early October in Paris were covered street lights and tiny gas curb lamps. "Genêt" ended with this optimistic thought: "With the danger past, the dimmed streets look very beautiful indeed."[131]

In the same issue of the *New Yorker*, satirist Howard Brubaker did not share the sentiments of his colleague in Paris. Great Britain and France received nothing at Munich other than Hitler's promise that the agreement ended his quest for territory, a promise which based "[o]n past performances ... is worth about as much as a last year's atlas." Referring to the infamous Chamberlain photograph upon his return from Munich, Brubaker wrote, "The Prime Minister was pretty lucky to get home with his umbrella." Due to the agreement, he believed that the United States remained a better place to live than Europe. Using his famous double-entendre, he stated that Americans did not allow "Pirates" to win unlike the English and French equating Nazis to the Pittsburgh baseball team that had just lost its bid for the National League pennant.[132]

In its editorial "Peace Is Ransomed," the *Baltimore Sun* expressed its disgust with the Munich dictate. No one could doubt the sincerity of Chamberlain and Daladier for attempting to preserve the peace, but they suffered a defeat by granting Hitler all his demands: "Neither Mr. Chamberlain and M. Daladier nor their nations ought to delude themselves ... that the substructure of permanent peace ... was established." According to the paper, the tense situation remained unresolved: "No basic problem has been solved, no cause of war removed. This is the fundamental fact of the agreement. Consequently, all talk about proceeding from this agreement to a general European agreement must be fantasy unless England and France are ready to acknowledge complete future subservience to Berlin."[133] In the same tone, the *New Republic* wondered: "Is international morality to be regarded henceforth as a myth?"[134]

Two days later, the *Los Angeles Times* reversed itself from many of its previous commentaries, offering a rather strange interpretation to the pact. Referring to editorials such as the *Baltimore Sun*'s piece and acknowledging that it had done its "share of criticising [sic]" the Western allies during the crisis, such critiques could not be true. According to the paper, the Munich Agreement made these views shallow and did great harm to the good reputations of the leaders of Britain and France. Rather, Chamberlain and Daladier were brave, intelligent men with great insight for their countries' futures, not cowards as many Americans and newspapers now portrayed them. Furthermore, Hitler had failed miserably since he was unable to immediately absorb the Sudetenland as he desired, but had to occupy it in stages under international scrutiny. As for the Czechoslovaks, they came out of the crisis rather well despite losing their border defenses and industrial complexes. They no longer possessed a disruptive element and had won the backing of powerful allies for guaranteeing the integrity of their new borders. The west coast daily concluded with an unusual thought asserting that Czechoslovakia "has lost some material defenses, but she has gained greatly in moral ones. She has lost some territory but she has gained enormously in prestige and in the esteem of the world."[135]

The staunchly conservative monthly *National Republic*, appropriately subtitled, *A Magazine of Fundamental Americanism*, presented an extreme isolationist viewpoint in its October editorial entitled "War Scare," obviously written before the agreement was reached. It expressed traditional American sentiments for the underdog, "Only an imbecile would fail to have great sympathy for Czechoslovakia in its recent predicament," quickly adding the caveat, "but our part should end there." The journal believed that the United States should not intervene actively abroad, and had shed blood needlessly in World War One causing subsequent government disorder and the great economic crisis still felt in 1938. It praised United States senators for keeping the country out of the World Court and the League of Nations. Lastly, implying that the Versailles Treaty was a travesty, it concluded its piece with an erroneous declaration since the League of Nations had nothing to do with the establishment of Czechoslovakia: "The creation of Czechoslovakia by the League twenty years ago was possibly a major error. It created a small nation that sooner or later was to become the prey of large nations. What is happening now in Czechoslovakia is merely a redeal of the population of the varied nationals then forcibly cut off from their original homelands."[136]

Clyde Eagleton, an international law professor and author,[137] analyzed American responses to the agreement in an article entitled "Aftermath of the 'Surrender' at Munich" that appeared in the November issue of *Independent Woman*. As others, he expressed relief that the crisis had ended, but noted that it had destroyed the post World War One settlements. He then delved into three viewpoints of the American people who saw the agreement as a German defeat, a worthy yet shameful abandonment to avoid war, or a total humiliating capitulation. He characterized the first as irrational since Hitler received what he wanted without firing a shot. As for the second, if people really believed it, peace remained wholly doubtful as the author noted, "Pandora's box has been opened and violent emotion and wild hopes have been released. Brute force has been successful and its results accepted...." He warned that Hitler would not be satisfied, and the only way to avoid war in face of his demands would be continued capitulation. Eagleton put no faith in the third ideal since to him it meant total passive resistance that would have to end at some time.

Eagleton viewed the "shameful surrender" at Munich as the result of a series of capitulations that would result in further aggression. Appeasement had begun earlier in the decade when the Western democracies and the League of Nations took little action when the Japanese violated several treaties by invading Manchuria in 1931. Although he claimed Great Britain and France could have easily stopped Japan, their inaction encouraged Italy's invasion of Ethiopia in 1935, Germany's various violations of the Treaty of Versailles, the Nazi seizure of Austria and the Sudetenland, and further Japanese aggression in China. Eagleton asked, "Who is to be next?"

Interestingly, the professor saw the Munich Pact as the result of broken treaties, failed international law, and shattered collective security rather than as a struggle between democracy and fascism. In his opinion, this was the traditional balance of power in action. The European balance shifted in favor of Germany and Japan as a result of Britain's and France's inaction. He compared the two Western democracies to law abiding people who, however, refuse to become involved when they witnessed a crime thereby actually further encouraging it. He warned, "The cost becomes greater with each incident and more incidents lie ahead."

Eagleton sarcastically admonished Americans who criticized Britain and France for their recent actions. Since the United States did not want to take any part in the crisis or in foreign affairs for the past twenty years, it should remain silent: "If any state in the world has failed in its responsibility for maintaining law and order, it is the United States." He believed that American inaction actually encouraged Great Britain to pursue appeasement at Munich. Eagleton blasted isolationism as a cause for the current tense state of the world:

> We can not have peace without paying for it. If we had aided to build—instead of leading the opposition against it—a strong international government (League of Nations), it might have been possible to repair the faults and errors of the Versailles system without resort to force; and if force had happened, it might have been possible to stop it in its earlier stages.

Although violence and lawlessness destroyed international cooperation and peace, he predicted the world would eventually return to them. Until then, "the prospect is disheartening." In the future, the United States would have two costly options: war or international cooperation. Until the country chose, Eagleton urged a military buildup to prepare for America's reentry into international affairs.[138]

Several sources also presented some rather strange twists to the pact. In its November issue, the *National Republic* in an editorial "Times Change" argued the Western democracies decided not to fight for Czechoslovakia because of its alliance with the USSR. Instead, Britain and France worked out the issue with Germany to undermine the Red menace in European affairs, hoping the Soviets would concentrate their efforts in Asia.[139]

The influential African-American weekly newspaper the *Pittsburgh Courier,* with a nationwide audience, remained silent throughout the crisis. Instead, it focused on issues important for its readership such as civil rights and the position of Africa in foreign affairs. Once the agreement had been reached, however, the weekly commented on the results. In a brief, scathing editorial entitled, "The 'Democracies' Save their Colonies," it opined that "England, France and their stooges" sacrificed Czechoslovakia "into the maw of the raging Nazi lion" to divert Hitler's desire for some of their profitable colonial possessions. Yet, the outcome at Munich had been predictable. The Western democracies established precedence with their earlier, passive stance in relation to the Italian invasion of Ethiopia: "After the betrayal of Ethiopia, it was to be expected that they would act similarly toward the Czechs." For the *Pittsburgh Courier*, however, the parallelism ended here. The Czechoslovaks, unlike the Ethiopians, gave up without firing a shot. The weekly concluded with a slap at Czechoslovakia, Britain, and France by asking, "Is this white supremacy?"[140]

A week later, on October 15, the same newspaper saw a conspiracy in the Munich Agreement that affected their co-nationals abroad. The meetings of the "so-called democracies" with "the gangster countries" at Munich secretly agreed to return Germany's colonies lost after World War One to Belgium, France, and Great Britain. Furthermore, in exchange for Italy withdrawing its "'volunteers'" from the Spanish Civil War, Britain and France would "recognize Italy's rape of Ethiopia and hail her half-pint king as Emperor." After discussing Europe's problems in Palestine and Asia, the editorial "New Deal In Colonies" concluded with a biting assessment of the white establishment: "This is white civilization and culture at work. It ought to prove instructive to the small minority of colored peoples who can't yet rid themselves of the notion that this civilization and culture is something to be worshiped."[141]

Opinion Polls

In their reports and opinions throughout the Munich crisis, newspapers and magazines presented the viewpoints of their parent organizations or owners. Consequently, they cannot always be counted as accurate barometers of sentiment. Perhaps a better indicator of American public opinion would be polls, although also not flawless, and at times difficult to interpret since anywhere between 3,000 and 50,000 people were interviewed per question.[142] The American Institute of Public Opinion, better known as the Gallup Poll, tallied surveys on the issues, underwritten by various larger newspapers across the political spectrum nationwide, for newspaper publication.[143] In the midst of the crisis when asked between September 15-20, "If England and France go to war against Germany do you think the US can stay out?" the responses proved isolationist with 57% yes and 43% no. Another poll conducted at the same time further exhibited strong isolationist sentiment. It showed Americans desiring a say in the war-making process: 68% believed that in order for war to be declared, with the exception of a national invasion, Congress needed the approval of the people through a national referendum. Such opinion eventually produced the failed Ludlow Amendment in January 1940.

As for the agreement itself, the organization queried people between October 3–8, 1938, releasing the results to the newspapers on October 14, 1938. Pollsters asked three questions: "Do you believe that England and France did the best thing in giving in to Germany instead of going to war?" "Do you think that Germany's demand for the annexation of the Sudeten German areas in Czechoslovakia was justified?" and "Do you think that this settlement (agreed to by England, France, and Germany) will result in peace for a number of years or in a greater possibility of war?" The poll concluded that Americans sympathized overwhelmingly with Czechoslovakia's plight (77% to 23%), opposing the incorporation of the Sudetenland into the Reich. Yet, a sizable majority (59% to 41%) believed that the Western democracies assumed the correct position in preserving the peace at the expense of Czechoslovakia. Nonetheless, attitudes about the future remained pessimistic, and continued to demonstrate the American public's schizophrenia toward foreign affairs. About the same amount of responses (60% to 40%) believed that Munich would not keep the peace,[144] while a November survey showed that 92% felt that Munich had not satisfied Hitler's territorial designs.[145] In related polls released in mid-October 1938, Americans remained somewhat confident that they could remain out of a European conflict. A slight majority (52% no, 48% yes) stated the United States would not have to fight Germany during their lifetimes. Despite this feeling of safety behind the oceans, Americans remained weary of the government's ability to stay out of conflicts in Europe and Asia as shown by their solid support for larger armies and navies with 71% and 65% yes responses respectively. These figures rose considerably by the end of the year to 86% and 82% in favor.[146]

Conclusion
Many world leaders and Americans erroneously believed the Munich Agreement would bring a lasting peace to Europe. The majority of American print media examined here shared this belief, yet, for the most part, it considered the pact a sell-out on the part of the Western democracies. The hope of a continued peace quickly dwindled in the months after the dictate, but Americans felt themselves safe from European events. Munich became a stopgap measure to buy time for Britain and France. These hopes were shattered with the final German destruction of rump Czechoslovakia in March 1939, and Nazi pres-

sure mounted on Poland. The great powers knew it would be a matter of time before the guns rang out again, which they did on September 1, 1939. In an editorial entitled, "The War the World Feared," from
September 2, 1939, the *Chicago Tribune* summed up what is considered the lesson of Munich:

> Hitler's statement of the immediate cause (of the invasion of
> Poland) might have seemed reasonable and convincing, but the
> world has a poor opinion of his good faith. His voice echoes in
> Austria and in Czecho-Slovakia.... The echo accuses him of per-
> fidy which he justifies as a means to an end. Perfidy is not a
> strange element in international relations. Hitler, however, has too
> much rejoiced in it. "Munich" is a word new within the last year
> in diplomatic language. Hitler has given it the significance and
> meaning it has. It spells betrayal.[147]

CHAPTER 3

REPORTING THE COLD WAR:

THE AMERICAN PRESS REPORTS THE

1948 COMMUNIST RISE TO POWER IN

CZECHOSLOVAKIA[1]

A. Paul Kubricht

Methodology

THIS CHAPTER examines the coverage of events during the communist rise to power in Czechoslovakia in February 1948 by popular American newspapers and news magazines. Closely linked to the communist takeover in February was Czechoslovak Foreign Minister Jan Masaryk's mysterious death in early March. Jan Masaryk's suicide, or assassination, added a tragic personal dimension to the politics of February. Speculation about the cause of his death kept Czechoslovakia in the headlines for several more weeks. This section explores the words and images regarding the state, culture, personalities, and events occurring in Czechoslovakia conveyed to the American reader during this time of international crisis.

The print media as defined herein includes news articles, editorials, columnist's opinion pieces, political cartoons, maps, and illustrations. The newspapers chosen to reflect a national readership were the *New York Times* and the *Christian Science Monitor*. Major regional newspapers evaluated were the *Chicago Tribune, Atlanta Constitution, San Francisco Chronicle, Chicago Daily News, St. Louis Globe-Democrat,* and *St. Louis Post-Dispatch*. In Chicago and St. Louis, competing newspapers were surveyed to explore variations in how different newspapers in one city presented events. The *Austin American* and *Austin Statesman* yielded additional reporting.

Time, Newsweek, and *U.S. News & World Report* (renamed from *United States News* in 1948) represent popular news journals. Magazines such as *Reader's Digest, American Mercury, Life,* and *Saturday Evening Post* tended to hold conservative and anti-communist orientations, while another group consisting of the *New Republic, Nation,* and *Commonweal* held the views of liberal Americans. This permitted a diversity of viewpoints across the political spectrum. It should be noted, however, that the most popular magazines in the United States at this time were not news-oriented.[2]

More specialized newspapers or magazines representing ethnic, religious, labor, or other narrower constituencies were consulted in passing. This group includes those journals or magazines which dealt specifically with international relations or current events such as *Foreign Affairs, The U.S. Department of State Bulletin, Foreign Policy Bulletin,* and *Current History* in spite of the narrow readership of these periodicals.

To gain a sense of continuity of American press coverage of events and life in Czechoslovakia, the review of selected newspapers begins in July 1947, when the Czechoslovak government reversed its decision to participate in the Marshall Plan. While the focal point of this chapter is 1948, the conflicts which occurred in the Cold War in the early summer 1947, influenced the perceptions of later political developments and reporting.

The examples of news and journalistic coverage which follow depict information and images about Czechoslovakia communicated to the American people. How Americans made decisions about international events during this stage of the Cold War is significant and controversial. Also relevant are the impact of the print media on politicians and other "elite" makers of foreign policy as well as attempts by politicians to influence press coverage. Debate concerning the effect of the print media on foreign policy and, in particular, the origins of the Cold War from 1945 to 1948 continues. The relationship between American public opinion and policy formulation, as well as how the foreign policy establishment disseminated its views and generated support for policy remain major issues in the context of the Cold War.[3] Certainly, policymakers of the United States did attempt to influence news coverage. For example, the *San Francisco*

Chronicle shifted to a more internationalist perspective after American diplomat, and father of the policy of containment of the Soviet Union, George F. Kennan visited with the editorial staff.[4]

General Observations of Press Coverage

The 1948 communist rise to power in Czechoslovakia influenced the developing American attitudes toward Soviet Russia and international communism during this stage of the Cold War. By 1948, Western and American suspicions of Soviet dictator Joseph Stalin and the Soviet Union had increased. Consequently, the print media supplied extensive coverage of the growing Soviet-American tension.[5] Many politicians and journalists looked for evidence that the Soviets indeed sought to increase their influence and control in Europe in addition to other parts of the world.

Newspaper coverage of events in Czechoslovakia varied, but it consistently contained more information and substance than that of the popular news magazines. The *New York Times* provided the most complete reporting of events in Czechoslovakia beginning in the summer 1947, when Czechoslovakia reversed its decision to participate in the Marshall Plan, until March 1948, when Jan Masaryk died. The paper also dealt more extensively with the events occurring in Czechoslovakia in the fall 1947, when communists challenged the independence of the Slovak Democratic party. The *New York Times* speculated on the shifting strategies of Premier Klement Gottwald and the Czechoslovak Communist party after he had attended a number of other meetings with East Central European communist leaders at this time. In late 1947, the paper reported that "the crisis in Czechoslovak affairs probably will come soon,"[6] and that "the final struggle is apparently now on, and moving rapidly to a decision."[7] In early February 1948, the *New York Times* published an editorial entitled "Dusk of Freedom in Prague."[8] From this ongoing coverage a regular reader would have some idea that the Czechoslovak Communist party had shifted its strategies and goals.

Most other newspapers tended to cover Czechoslovakia from a crisis perspective. Some carried articles dealing with the Czechoslovak government's decision to forgo participation in the Marshall Plan, but, in general, reporting of Czechoslovakia remained sporadic until the start of the February 1948 crisis. For this reason, most readers would have little understanding of the background of the February

1948 events. Many readers would have picked up their papers in February, and suddenly read about a belligerent Soviet state not only challenging the freedom of democratic Czechoslovakia, but also apparently threatening to dominate all of Europe.

Regional news coverage of the events surrounding the communist coup and Jan Masaryk's death varied. The *Chicago Tribune* published fewer editorials and news articles than any of the major regional newspapers. However, the Chicago source did publish more political cartoons related to the crisis than most of the other newspapers. The *Chicago Tribune*'s rival, the *Chicago Daily News*, contained more news of the crisis, including more on-the-scene reporting, and also gave the crisis greater headline emphasis. The *Chicago Tribune* consistently gave the coup a secondary headline with the major headline focusing on local news. The *San Francisco Chronicle* contained the most complete coverage of any of the regional papers; it included articles, news analysis, editorials, and also personal interviews with prominent Czechoslovaks. Much of the coverage in the various newspapers was similar, based on news service reports; in some cases, the same correspondent's report surfaced in different papers. The *Christian Science Monitor*, while not having the quantity of articles, tended to present longer, more descriptive and analytical reporting.

Naturally, weekly news magazines gave weekly summaries. These articles lacked the analytical depth of newspaper coverage and analysis by columnists. *U.S. News & World Report* had lengthier articles, but communicated an apocalyptic spirit of coming war and imminent doom. The liberal magazines, while expressing sorrow, tended to blame Washington for the events in Czechoslovakia.

Non-news oriented magazines seldom dealt with the crisis or politics of the situation specifically. They presented idyllic images of Czechoslovakia such as baroque architecture, majestic castles, and dancing peasants in native costume. Even after the coup, the reader would not have sensed the major political upheaval which had just occurred.

Stereotyping the Nation-State
News reporting, including international crises, deals with words and images. In covering such stories, reporters must separate their personal beliefs and experiences from the story reported. Recent foreign policy studies relating to gender provide one example of how lan-

guage influences policy.[9] With these factors in mind, this study examines the beliefs, values, and assumptions expressed, not only about individuals or events, but also attitudes concerning a people, a culture, and a state. In the case of Czechoslovakia, the American press used certain events, concepts, and words to describe this particular nation-state or group of peoples.[10] The perception of how the news-reading public and government officials viewed Czechoslovakia influenced American reactions and responses to the 1948 February revolution. In addition, how readers regarded the developing Cold War and the relationship between the Soviet Union and the United States influenced American reactions to the incidents in Czechoslovakia.

As the crisis of February 1948 developed, news reporting portrayed Czechoslovakia four major ways: a small country surrounded by aggressive communists and caught in the middle of a great power struggle; a liberal democracy with Western traditions; an innocent victim of aggression forced to experience a situation remarkably similar to the events of Munich 1938; and a country led by and populated with political realists. American readers encountered these images or stereotypes of Czechoslovakia as the February crisis grew. Often a simplified interpretation of historical events formed the basis of these characterizations, but more important than the actual incident became the perception or stereotype that developed from the event and how the newspaper presented it to its reading public.

First, the print media often portrayed Czechoslovakia as a small or "little" country mostly surrounded by communist states with the great power of the Soviet Union lurking nearby. For example, the *Austin Statesman* referred to "little Czechoslovakia"[11] and the *Chicago Daily News* wrote that "the Red Army surrounds the country on all sides."[12] Although a reality of the post-World War Two situation, portraying the country as "small" had also been part of Czechoslovakia's description in 1938. Instead of the great power Germany, Czechoslovakia now faced the Soviet Union. *New York* Times reporter James Reston wrote that "strategically Czechoslovakia is surrounded."[13] One editorial argued that "geography played a fateful role" in life of this small nation.[14] Readers would also realize this fact if, and when, they studied the maps depicting the situation in which Czechoslovakia found itself.[15] Political cartoons often depicted Czechoslovakia as a small man while representing the Soviet Union as something large, such as Stalin's giant-sized pipe or an enormous bear.[16]

In communicating smallness and the implicit weakness of Czechoslovakia, the traditional American sympathy for the underdog became apparent. For example DeWitt MacKenzie of the *Austin Statesman* characterized Czechoslovakia as "a valiant, but tiny state" resisting Soviet expansionism.[17] Comments such as "poor little Czechoslovakia"[18] or "small, isolated nations create a vacuum"[19] typify this perception. Czechoslovakia's diminutive size evoked a sense of tragedy or misfortune.

The second theme running through the sources linked Czechoslovakia with Western liberal democracy. The *New York Times* wrote in an editorial that "the history of modern Europe might be written in terms of Czechoslovakia's struggle to be free...."[20] Papers described Czechoslovakia as a "freedom loving little nation,"[21] its populace as "a sensitive, freedom-loving people,"[22] and a nation possessing a "tough-fibered" democracy.[23] San Francisco newspaperman Drew Pearson wrote that the founders of Czechoslovakia, Thomas G. Masaryk and Edvard Beneš, created a "vigorous republic."[24]

Liberal writers also shared this belief. *Nation* described Czechoslovakia as having a "long democratic tradition,"[25] and as a people bred in the democratic tradition.[26] The *New Republic* referred to "traditional Czech democratic principles."[27] Historian Hans Kohn, writing in *Current History*, described the Czechs as steeped in the Western tradition of liberty and freedom which he saw going back to the political leadership of the nineteenth and early twentieth centuries: František Palacký, Karel Havlíček, and Thomas G. Masaryk.[28]

Seeing Czechoslovakia as a freedom-loving republic naturally led to the idea that this democratic orientation engendered a special relationship with the United States. For example, the *New York Times* characterized Czechoslovaks as a "people ... friendly" to the United States.[29] It also quoted a Czech as saying that because of the First Czechoslovak Republic, the country had become more Western than Eastern.[30] A writer in the *New Republic* stated that "the Czechs consider themselves Westerners," and that "personal property is as sacred to them as it is to us in the United States."[31] Editorials in the *Chicago Daily News* noted that the United States had ties with Czechoslovakia going back to World War One and President Woodrow Wilson, and that "the United States has a personal interest in Czechoslovakian affairs because of the American background of President Beneš and Foreign Minister Jan Masaryk."[32] Throughout C.L. Sulzberger's interview with Edvard Beneš, the Czechoslovak president constantly asserted Czechoslovakia's Western orientation, especially in culture and commerce, in spite of its growing special political relationship with Moscow and at a time when Soviet domination of other East Central European countries was occurring.[33] The *Chicago Tribune* compared the Czechoslovak people to Americans with "ties of blood and republican traditions."[34] An editorial in the *St. Louis Globe-Democrat* stated that "their ties with America are strong—The Czech constitution was written in Pittsburgh."[35] Writers in various newspapers frequently mentioned the American origins of the First Czechoslovak Republic. Even after the crisis, the *New Republic* continued to report that "most Czechs retain an underlying warm feeling for America."[36] While political cartooning did not focus on this categorization, one, particularly powerful, showed the ghost of President Woodrow Wilson accompanying President Beneš who carried the lifeless body of Czechoslovak democracy (see Figure 11, Chapter 6).[37]

The memory of appeasement and misfortune emanating from the 1938 Munich Conference characterizes the coverage of the third media focus. Repeatedly, the situation of February 1948 was seen as an opportunity for the West to apply the lessons that Munich should have taught. Writers readily drew similarities between 1948 and 1938. Until February 1948, the print media discussed Munich purely as a historic event in Czechoslovakia's past. However, as soon as it became clear that a communist coup had occurred, analogies to Munich and the "spirit of Munich" became much more commonplace.

Editorials and news columnists made the most frequent parallels to Munich. An editorial in the *Chicago Tribune* entitled "Full Circle" regarded the current events as a rerun of 1938, and speculated which country would fall to communism after Czechoslovakia.[38] Others commented that since Munich, Czechoslovakia could not really trust its friends in the West,[39] and that February 1948 compared to Hitler's territorial aggressions.[40] One newspaper stated that the events provided another example of what happens to small nations.[41] A different writer spoke of another "Czech Tragedy."[42] Newspaper editorials consistently returned to the Munich crisis for lessons to guide Washington's response in 1948.

Readers also saw references and allusions to Munich in headlines on the front page and in the opening paragraphs of news stories. Examples include: "Beneš Accused Czech Premier of Hitler Talk,"[43]

"Britain Recalls Munich,"[44] and "Strong Policy or Another Munich, Says Morse."[45] These and other articles quoted prominent American politicians and international statesmen, such as Anthony Eden and Georges Bidault, British and French politicians respectively, making parallels to Munich. A reader could not escape the impression that Stalin and Soviet Russia were imitating Hitler and Nazi Germany. The question remained whether the West would respond more decisively than it had in 1938 and 1939.

Columnists in newspapers and magazines also made comparisons to Munich. *Chicago Daily News* writer David Lawrence in "A Tragic Parallel" compared Stalin's aggression to Hitler's "grab of state after state,"[46] and in a later column he observed Stalin making the same mistake as Hitler.[47] Dorothy Thompson, also of the *Chicago Daily News*, referred to Jan Masaryk as being "wounded to the heart by Munich," implying that those events in 1938 had so scared and shaped him that, by 1948, it would influence his response to the current crisis.[48] George E. Sokolsky, of the *St. Louis Globe-Democrat*, criticized the Western lack of will as in 1938, and raised the issue of appeasement again in later pieces.[49]

In addition to newspapers, frequent allusions to Munich appeared in magazines and periodicals. *Newsweek*, referring to Munich, stated that "last week, totalitarianism struck down Czechoslovakia once more."[50] *Life* made the comparison to Hitler's takeover.[51] Liberal periodicals also mentioned Munich. The *New Republic* reported that "Czech democrats, remembering Munich and the Nazi occupation, put up a fight to save civil liberties."[52] *Nation* took a different slant by reflecting on Stalin's earlier support for Czechoslovakia during the Munich crisis in 1938, and speculated about what was happening to the cooperation between Czechoslovak democrats and communists that had evolved in the period from 1938 to 1948.[53] Both conservatives and liberals worried about the Munich parallels. However, conservatives saw it as an issue of aggressive communism while liberals focused more on American policy failures that led to another Munich-like crisis.

A number of editorial page cartoons also dealt with the Munich legacy. The *New York Times* ran one entitled "Another Lesson From Adolf" with Hitler's ghost lurking behind Stalin and Beneš.[54] One cartoon had a large boot sporting a Soviet hammer and sickle stepping behind a footprint embedded with Hitler's name.[55] "A Decade of Dignity" portrayed Beneš both in 1938 and 1948 facing first Nazi and then communist demands (see Figure 10, Chapter 6).[56] It would be hard for a reader to escape analogies between the two events separated by a decade.

The last characterization of Czechoslovakia, less overt than the previous three, represented Czechoslovakia and its democratic leadership as pragmatists. The *San Francisco Chronicle* exemplified this type of reporting, "In modern times, the Czechs have been realists rather than romantics when faced with almost hopeless situations."[57] Some writers commented that in dealing with the great powers Czechoslovakia manifested a "well known sense of realism."[58] Such remarks implied that after World War Two, Beneš and the Czechoslovak leaders "chose what they considered a realistic compromise."[59]

A review of these four stereotypes of Czechoslovakia by the press in the United States finds they are generally positive representations and embody values which resonate with the American people's support of democracy and fair play, concern for the "little guy," and belief in political pragmatism. With so much in common, immediate American involvement to uphold these shared ideals might be expected. Certainly no other country in East Central Europe identified as much with American traditions and values.

Stereotyping National Leadership

During the months surrounding the events of 1948, the American print media wrote about a number of Czechoslovak leaders, discussing their personalities, beliefs, and contributions. The most frequent subjects were President Edvard Beneš and Foreign Minister Jan Masaryk. In articles containing some historical analysis, the founder and first president of the First Czechoslovak Republic, Thomas G. Masaryk, was mentioned as well. Increasingly, the sources observed the virtues and weaknesses of the leader of the Czechoslovak Communist party, Klement Gottwald. During 1947 and 1948, the names of other Czechoslovak political leaders, both communist and democratic, appeared, although with very little analysis of their policies or personal background. The one possible exception was Zdeněk Fierlinger, a controversial leader of the Czechoslovak Social Democratic party, who cooperated with the communists in their rise to power.

The events surrounding the founding of the First Republic during World War One in Pittsburgh, Pennsylvania, linked President Edvard Beneš to the United States.[60] Both he and Thomas G. Masaryk were associated with President Woodrow Wilson, the American president at the time of the Pittsburgh Pact. As such, the image of Beneš as a "Wilsonian Democrat" held strong. As mentioned earlier, one political cartoon particularly communicated this spirit of kinship by having the ghost of Wilson accompanying Beneš as he carried the body of Czech national democracy (see Figure 11, Chapter 6).[61] Clearly American readers saw an image of Beneš as a leader within the American democratic political tradition, a man who enjoyed reading American (and British) books and the life and culture offered by the West.

However, as the February crisis commenced, the *New York Times* portrayed Beneš as a "wily little" man.[62] As a realist,[63] he not only promoted democratic traditions in Czechoslovakia, but also held a vision of a united Europe,[64] and, yet, he could still navigate around the dangers created by the Cold War and the increasingly acrimonious confrontation between the communist and capitalist systems. The print media presented Beneš as diplomatically adept, and certainly helped promote the image of him as a person who could bridge the differences between East and West. Most of the press wrote approvingly of his support for socialist economic programs for Czechoslovakia as a realistic way of facing the post-World War Two world.

Nevertheless, as the communists gained influence during the February days, conservative columnists, in particular, began to question his insight and realism. Descriptions of Beneš as "aging,"[65] "weepy,"[66] a "foolish visionary,"[67] "bewildered," and "beaten down,"[68] as well as in doubtful health physically and emotionally appeared in news reports.[69] Increasingly, the sources portrayed him as a tragic and humiliated figure rather than a visionary realist. In fact, the word "tragedy" became more frequently associated with him. On an individual level, events had turned these days into a personal misfortune and not just a national or world tragedy.

Right-wing commentators grew more critical of Beneš as the crisis progressed. Syndicated columnists Joseph and Stewart Alsop wrote that Beneš had been warned over five years earlier that Czechoslovak Defense Minister General Ludvík Svoboda began infiltrating communists into the army.[70] For these writers, the coup demonstrated that one could not parley with the deceptive and scheming Soviets; therefore, all of Beneš's negotiations proved "futile." In the *St. Louis Globe-Democrat* George E. Sokolsky argued that Beneš paid for his misjudgments and efforts to "do the impossible," i.e. negotiate with communists.[71] The Czechoslovaks now reaped the consequences of serving "as the diplomatic valet" to the Soviets, and Beneš, personally, paid for gambling "everything upon Josef Stalin's personal pledge."[72] Beneš, the cagey negotiator, had become Beneš the aging and naive dupe. Even the *New York Times* wrote that "this ideological Garden of Eden has proved to be a fool's paradise."[73]

Another more isolated charge raised in headlines screamed "Benes Said To Have Been Secret Agent For Stalin," and was followed by a secondary headline reading "Soviet Document in State Department Reported to Show Czech President Made Deal With Red Marshal."[74] The article discussed a supposed June 25, 1941 secret treaty Beneš signed with Stalin. According to the piece, Czechoslovakia would "act as Russia's spearhead in Western Europe," Soviet Russia would be permitted to annex Ruthenia, and, in return, Czechoslovakia could exile its German and Hungarian minorities. The news report portrayed Beneš as having "bargained away his soul" and therefore Czechoslovakia "cannot complain that it was sold down the river." [75] A book published almost fifty years after the 1948 events by a former Soviet secret police NKVD official has also stated that Beneš escaped from Czechoslovakia to Britain using NKVD money, that the NKVD highly influenced him, and that Beneš had "become our agent in 1938."[76]

The other major Czechoslovak figure appearing in the headlines these days was Foreign Minister Jan Masaryk, the son of the founder of Czechoslovakia. His sudden death under tragic and mysterious circumstances led to speculation whether he committed suicide or had been assassinated. Masaryk had many American ties: his mother was an American, he had married an American, he had worked in America, and later visited many times. He was clearly at ease with Americans and American culture. As a genuine extrovert, he enjoyed relationships with many Americans, including journalists who repaid him with a largely favorable press. Following his death, it seemed that Masaryk had talked "in confidence" to almost every reporter of note. A number of writers recalled some story or personal opinion of Masaryk's that they could now relate due to his passing.

Reporters also often described him as a sophisticated cosmopolitan using such words like "playboy," "shrewd," and "witty" while sometimes employing off-color terms.[77] He was said to be "fond of girls and gambling," and that he "loved the good life, silk pajamas, civilized people, simple food and Scotch whiskey."[78] Whether these flamboyant images fitted the Puritan streak in America remains doubtful, but writers certainly appreciated his earthiness. His death triggered an evaluation and reassessment of his political contributions. Portrayed as a fighter for liberty, equality, and justice,[79] Masaryk would not sell his soul and mind.[80] A caption of a picture described him as a "Symbol of Democracy and Freedom."[81]

Again, as they had with Beneš, writers, and conservatives in particular, raised questions about Masaryk's political judgment. One column headline read "Masaryk Praises Russia, Gives His Full Approval To Czech Red Coup."[82] A columnist regarded him as "a sort of latterday Schweik."[83] However, most of the analysis of Masaryk came immediately after his death. The crisis coverage linked his name with Beneš's, but did not focus on him or his role. The first reports of his death dealt with it as a suicide, but gradually as peculiar details became known, the widely discussed possibility of assassination appeared. Some political cartoons dealing with his death presented a spectral quality (see Figure 9, Chapter 6 for an example).[84]

When Masaryk received negative treatment, news sources ascribed character deficiencies such as "opportunist,"[85] or suggested timidity, or even cowardice.[86] A columnist also compared Masaryk to Henry A. Wallace, a liberal Democrat challenging Harry S Truman for the presidency.[87] Given the charged atmosphere at the start of the 1948 presidential race where many portrayed Wallace, at best, as an unwitting stooge of Moscow, such a comparison could not be a positive one. In response to conservative attacks on Masaryk's willingness to work with communists, radio broadcaster Edward R. Murrow attacked the Alsops for referring "to Jan Masaryk as 'the salon favorite in New York, who has played perhaps the most morally shabby game of all.'" For Murrow, Masaryk was a great man who faced pressures and decisions that should not be second-guessed.[88]

Newspapers referred less frequently to the communist leaders of Czechoslovakia. They were certainly not portrayed in the personal depth of Beneš or Masaryk, but tended to be depicted as crude and anti-intellectual or in the case of previously mentioned Social Democrat Zdeněk Fierlinger, an unscrupulous opportunist. Papers regarded Klement Gottwald, the leader of the Czechoslovak Communist party, as unquestionably obedient to Joseph Stalin; one article even mentioned that Gottwald resembled Stalin and behaved with a "calm and deliberate" demeanor similar to the Soviet dictator.[89] Following the

Czechoslovak agreement to participate in the Marshall Plan, the *New York Times* reported that Stalin gave Gottwald a tongue lashing, forcing him to reverse the decision.[90] During the fall 1947, he was portrayed as doing the bidding of Moscow. As the February crisis developed, reporting showed Gottwald as treating Beneš with nothing but contempt as he tried to "beat down" the president and "break the necks" of Beneš's supporters.[91] Another article quoted Gottwald as describing Beneš "as a little Czech teacher with the ambitions of a Napoleon." [92] In a more positive manner, a piece described Gottwald as "a mild-mannered, pipe-smoking man in his home or office."[93] However, even this writer went on to say that before a crowd "he swings his arms and bellows."[94] Another article even referred to his wife as a "robust red," a judicious way of depicting her.[95] The print media ignored or simplistically presented the complexities of Gottwald's personality and his political maneuverings.[96] Clearly American reporters had not come to grips with Gottwald's character, and he seemed an unknown quantity to them.

The Role of the Czechoslovak Crisis in the Beginning of the Cold War

The Czechoslovak coup played a significant role at the start of the Cold War, contributing to an escalating hostility and wariness in the relations between the United States and the Soviet Union. The impact of the February events have often been neglected because of the intensity of other Cold War confrontations that took place before and after the crisis. The Czechoslovak revolution occurred in the midst of communist threats to Greece and Turkey in 1947 leading to the Truman Doctrine, the Marshall Plan, the Berlin Airlift, and communist victories resulting in the takeover of China in 1949. It took place at a time when many in America began reassessing the intentions of the Soviet Union and its role in world politics, and what the appropriate response of the United States should be.

While some newspaper reports indicated prior to February that communists in Czechoslovakia were preparing to challenge the government, most Americans expressed surprise at the events. As has been noted earlier, most papers, with the exception of the *New York Times*, gave few indications of an imminent communist seizure of power. Most readers would not have read much about Czechoslovakia since the summer 1947, when the Czechoslovak government changed its decision to participate in the Marshall Plan. While that event concerned many Americans, Beneš's government seemed to continue conducting its affairs as usual.

During 1947, accounts of Soviet pressures and communist takeovers in other East Central European states had been reported, but somehow Czechoslovakia appeared different. The widespread perception saw Czechoslovakia as a nation with a strong democratic political tradition. People wanted to believe that Beneš's balancing act between East and West would succeed. The situation in Czechoslovakia just did not seem as relevant or grave as events occurring in Germany, the eastern Mediterranean, or in the growing communist vote in France and Italy. Yet, when the crisis occurred, it concentrated America's focus on the issue of the real intentions of the Soviet Union, and led to what some call "The War Scare of 1948."

From the press coverage, several issues of the Czechoslovak coup clearly had a pivotal impact on American foreign policy. The crisis raised questions about America's will to resist the spread of totalitarian government and the policies pursued by Washington regarding relations with Stalin. The takeover created an image of an expansionist and aggressive Soviet state and ended any hopes of "bridge-building" between the forces of democratic capitalism and communism. Furthermore, it helped secure the passage of the Marshall Plan in Congress, and it undermined Henry A. Wallace's bid for the Democratic nomination for president. In the immediate wake of the coup, war alarms went off. However, it did not lead to the commitment of American military force or even assertive diplomatic action by the United Nations to restore Czechoslovakia to its previous political situation.

The print media resurrected 1938 as it tried to assess an appropriate American response to the Soviet takeover. As the crisis progressed with an apparent lack of any United States action, the question arose of whether the same mistake was being made with Stalin as had been made with Hitler at Munich. To many the lesson of 1938 clearly taught that appeasement would not halt aggression.[97] A number of political cartoons depicted this viewpoint.[98] A column by David Lawrence in *US News & World Report* proved to be the one exception to the 1938 comparison when he argued that 1948 was not like 1938. He noted that the Western democracies had grown stronger and more able to respond to aggression.[99] Writers also raised questions about whether President Franklin D. Roosevelt's World

War Two Soviet policy contributed to the coup. Controversy erupted over the American army's failure to liberate Prague when its
troops occupied Pilsen, Czechoslovakia, at the end of the war.[100] The
implication arose that if General Dwight D. Eisenhower had moved
American troops into the heart of Czechoslovakia, the world would
not be facing the events of 1948.

Print media coverage, with the exception of the liberal magazines
such as the *New Republic*, overwhelmingly described the Soviets as
aggressive expansionists seeking to dominate Europe. Headlines
appeared such as "Soviet Push Westward Long in the Making,"[101] "Trying to Complete Red Domination of Eastern Europe,"[102] and "How
Far West Can The Communist Drive Go Without Major Collision?"[103]
Several papers contained an article written by Stanisław Mikołajcyzk,
a former prime minister of Poland, arguing that Czechoslovakia had
become the Soviet first step with France and Italy next.[104] Other
reporters also expressed a rising concern about what countries the
Soviets would subsequently take.[105] Americans assumed that the
Soviets would keep on seizing territory, but where would the Kremlin strike next? The Alsops' column particularly supported this
theme.[106] A large number of political cartoons portrayed Joseph
Stalin and Soviet Russia as greedy land grabbers (see Figure 6, Chapter 6 for an example).[107]

However, other reports stressed the Soviets had moved into
Czechoslovakia because of weakness.[108] Columnist David Lawrence
asserted that Moscow's move into Czechoslovakia resulted from fear,
and that it would find itself in an "economic mess" due to the
takeover. He speculated that it might even lead to internal dissension
within the Soviet Union.[109] Henry A. Wallace, echoing this view, stated that "Russia is terribly afraid,"[110] while those magazines associated
with liberal America also followed this argument.[111]

Until the Czechoslovak crisis occurred, the Marshall Plan had been
stalled in a Congress unwilling to increase government spending. An
editorial in the *San Francisco Chronicle* called the Marshall Plan
America's "best hope" to preserve freedom in Europe.[112] A later editorial stated that the Marshall Plan was "our sole hope," and without
it the United States "will lose Western Europe."[113] It noted that Congress sped up its consideration of the Marshall Plan as a result of the
coup.[114] The "Whispers Column" in *U.S. News & World Report* stated that Stalin's actions had added one billion dollars to the Marshall

Plan,[115] while the press regularly quoted Michigan Senator Arthur H. Vandenberg as justifying the need for the Marshall Plan, and urging the need to speed up aid.[116]

While the Truman administration finally gained Congressional approval for the Marshall Plan in April, critics of the policy did exist. The *Chicago Tribune*, while maintaining staunch opposition to communist tactics in Czechoslovakia, tried to keep from linking the crisis to the need for increased economic aid to Europe. Several newspapers carried Ohio Senator Robert A. Taft's opposition to spending for the Marshall Plan.[117] A column by George Weller argued that Czechoslovakia's fall "punctures the chief argument supporting the Marshall Plan." The "Czechs were well-fed and still succumbed to communism." Interestingly, an editorial appearing on the same page attacked Weller's position.[118] Nevertheless, within a month of the crisis a Republican dominated Congress had agreed to support the Marshall Plan.

Henry A. Wallace, a prominent liberal preparing to challenge Harry S Truman as the Democratic party's nominee in the November elections, soon found himself mired in controversy as a result of the events of 1948. In foreign policy he argued for better relations with the Soviet Union, and presented the case that Washington's increasingly strident anti-communism caused American-Soviet relations to deteriorate. In the case of the Czechoslovak crisis, Wallace charged that it occurred when the United States organized a right-wing coup which forced Moscow to react.[119] He referred back to a statement made on February 20, 1948, by the American ambassador to Czechoslovakia in which the envoy stated he hoped that Czechoslovakia would still participate in the Marshall Plan, knowing that this meant communists would have to be excluded from the government for this to happen. The *Atlanta Constitution* also quoted Wallace as saying that "if he had been in President Truman's shoes he might have prevented the Communist coup in Czechoslovakia."[120] For the presidential hopeful, the issue became how Washington would feel if Moscow began to try to influence events in Cuba.

Columnists, in particular, began to stress Wallace's naivete in thinking communists would cooperate toward common goals. Newspaperman Drew Pearson felt that Wallace needed to realize the impossibility of working with the Soviets, since cooperation was "a two-way street."[121] Edgar Mowrer wrote an editorial in the *San Francisco* Chronicle entitled "Masaryk and Henry Wallace. The Error of

Trusting Russia."[122] He accused Wallace, like Jan Masaryk, of being "hopelessly obtuse on one subject, the Soviet Union," and believing that everything would be perfectly fine if the United States just left Soviet Russia alone. While not mentioning Wallace specifically, an editorial in the *St. Louis Globe-Democrat* stressed that "Czechoslovakia's tragic plight is a pat example of what happens when any country believes it can collaborate with Russia and preserve its own freedom."[123] In the same paper, George E. Sokolsky linked Wallace to appeasement.[124] The Alsops stressed the "futility" of working with the Soviets,[125] while Leland Stowe, in the *St. Louis Post-Dispatch*, argued that liberals should open their eyes.[126]

The liberal media defended Wallace's position and ideas by tending to see Moscow being pushed into its decisions by narrow and short-sighted American policy.[127] Some saw the angry response of Secretary of State James F. Byrnes to the applause given by two Czechoslovak communist officials for Andrei Vyshinsky, the Soviet Deputy Minister for Foreign Affairs, as thoughtless and narrow-minded.[128] However, the largely anti-Wallace, pro-Washington rhetoric of the mainline press drowned these opinions.

The most alarming result of the coup and Jan Masaryk's death became the spread of the belief that war with the Soviet Union loomed or at least would occur within the year.[129] Initially, the concern focused on continued Soviet growth into Western Europe or Finland. By March, headlines and news articles warned that if the United States did not stop Soviet expansion, world revolution and communist domination would be inevitable.[130] American policy was being tested, and it remained to be seen if Washington's response would be strong enough. A number of columnists also added to the war scare.[131] Secretary of State George C. Marshall's statement about the world situation being very serious further increased the alarm.[132]

The Americans responded with overwhelming sympathy to the situation in Czechoslovakia and to the plight of the Czechoslovak peoples. Great shock and fear occurred; yet, the reaction of the United States to Soviet aggressiveness remained only rhetoric even in spite of the fact that many felt a hot, shooting war might soon occur. While print media reaction in America expressed great indignation and even fear for the future, no one called for the United States to respond with force. It might even be questioned how aggressively Washington pursued diplomatic pressure, because it was Chile that brought the issue of the February coup before the United Nations. Both the press and government officials quoted earlier recognized that Czechoslovakia, and in particular Beneš and Masaryk, had a special relationship with the Soviet Union which limited the Czechoslovak freedom to maneuver and hampered an American response. This predicament had been made clear when Czechoslovakia had to reverse its decision to enter the Marshall Plan in July 1947. However, the American press and people somehow wanted to believe that freedom would exist in Czechoslovakia as long as Prague did nothing to antagonize Moscow.

Several papers quoted Washington officials as having "long expected the Communists to seize open control in Prague.... the only surprise is that the Kremlin has waited so long to act."[133] A journalist summarized this feeling when he wrote that "American policy in Europe during this period has recognized the right of Russia to have 'friendly governments' along her European frontier," but Moscow has turned them into "controlled governments."[134] Even before the takeover, suspicions arose about Soviet impending actions.[135] Yet, if the United States did not respond before a Soviet move, it would be less likely that Washington would act after any Soviet activity. Maps, used in newspapers months before the February coup to indicate areas under Soviet control, had regularly included Czechoslovakia.[136]

American press coverage of the increased international tension forced American readers to consider what would happen after Czechoslovakia's fall to communism. However, it became clear that if the United States stood firm against the spread of communism, it would be in Western Europe or some other area of the world and not Czechoslovakia. Washington would not choose Czechoslovakia as the location to resist Soviet expansionism in spite of the largely positive feelings about its people and leaders. Czechoslovakia was not perceived as vital to American interests. Earlier in Turkey in 1946, Washington had opposed anticipated Soviet expansionism, and Stalin had learned to keep a "watchful eye on the dangers of escalation."[137] While Stalin had become more calculating of how far his actions could go before eliciting an American response from the 1946 Turkey crisis, in the case of Czechoslovakia in 1948, Washington sent no signals that Soviet moves would be challenged by military force or diplomatic threats. The result was a Stalinist client regime in Czechoslovakia.

Although it displayed strengths and weaknesses in its treatment of events in Czechoslovakia, the print media managed to describe the major developments of the crisis, but was less enlightening regarding the developments leading to the February coup. However, neither Washington nor the American public seemed prepared or willing to prevent the rise of a communist-dominated government in Czechoslovakia. In fact, it might be argued, given the predominance of anti-Soviet rhetoric in so much of the coverage, the print media failed to create a greater sense of public outcry regarding the events in Czechoslovakia.

CHAPTER 4

AMERICAN NEWSPAPER MEDIA PORTRAYAL

OF THE 1968 PRAGUE SPRING

James W. Peterson

Significance of the Prague Spring

WHEN CZECHOSLOVAKIA exploded in reform in 1968 and experienced the shock of the Warsaw Pact invasion, most observers interpreted the Prague Spring as an isolated series of events unusual for that country. Analysts saw continuity between the level of Soviet control prior to the year 1968 and the re-imposition of restrictions after August 1968. The Czechoslovak reform movement proved merely a blip on the horizon and a non-repeatable event, at least in that "normalized"[1] country. The Prague Spring invited that type of interpretation because the Czechoslovak citizenry had previously endured twenty years under Soviet-style communism. After the end of World War Two, Czechoslovakia succumbed to rule by the Communist party. The 1948 communist coup betrayed the interwar democratic experiment of the First Czechoslovak Republic. Although the Czechoslovak Communist party had a large following in the 1945–48 period, the establishment of the Gottwald[2] regime appeared to most observers as an imposition by Moscow. A clear imitation of patterns in the Soviet Union with respect to centralization of the economy, de-emphasis on the organs of the official government, restrictions on the press, reliance on the party as the effective replacement for the state organs of power, and assertion of cultural controls followed in Czechoslovakia. The purges in the early 1950s became especially shocking in a nation that prided itself on a long history of civility.

Little changed with the advent to power of Antonín Novotný in 1953. While Poland and Hungary in their own individual ways made efforts to modify the excesses of their communist regimes in 1956, Czechoslovakia under Novotný remained the same.[3] As Josip Broz Tito of Yugoslavia challenged Soviet leadership within the bloc all during the 1950s and 1960s, leaders of the Czechoslovak Communist party remained close to Moscow. Even East Germany began a meaningful economic reform movement in 1962, not duplicated in nearby Czechoslovakia, while Romanian leadership in the mid-1960s became quite maverick in foreign policy. The unyielding nature of the Czechoslovak Communist party permitted no challenges or reforms before 1968.

The Prague Spring reforms centered on four overlapping areas of change. They included significant modification of the political system, new patterns of management of the economy, adjustments in the legal-constitutional system, and an altered federal relationship between Czechs and Slovaks.

The political goals of the Prague Spring reformers were diverse. First, the leadership intended to reduce the level of party intervention in the government. Related goals included an overall upgrading of the government, its ministries, the presidency, the national legislature: the National Assembly, the sham political coalition controlled by the Communist party: the National Front, and Slovak institutions. In particular, the National Assembly would receive significant legislative powers. These new powers would include stronger legislative committees, extended debate on major legislative issues, and meaningful oversight of governmental ministers. A changed Communist party was also part of the plan. Abolition of the *nomenklatura*, the communist elite patronage system, would enable the party to bring in a wider range of people and skills. Control over regional and district party appointments would reside primarily at the local level rather than within the Central Committee, the policy making body of the party. Draft statutes for a new party constitution guaranteed a minority the right to formulate its viewpoints and to have them published in the minutes.[4] Further, in April, Alexander Dubček, the First Secretary of the Communist Party of Czechoslovakia, called for creation of an atmosphere in which criticism of party officials would be acceptable.[5] The April Action Program envisioned the party's role as one of "arousing socialist initiative" instead of one being the overall caretaker of society.[6]

Economic changes constituted a second major area of reform during the Prague Spring. Whereas the State Planning Commission had previously dominated the policy area, reformers intended to reduce its role to that of a regular ministry. This would obviously entail a sharp reduction in its power to enforce an overall plan with quotas for the entire economy. The leadership would additionally experiment with worker councils that would have the power to name and dismiss their directors.[7] Concrete economic changes also included price reforms. The proportion of free prices would be higher and the percentage of fixed prices lower. Although modest, such alterations would be a marked departure from past practice.[8]

A third area of reform covered the legal-constitutional sphere. In February 1968, a sweeping statement called for rehabilitation of all previous victims of the Nazi and communist eras. In April, however, the reformers narrowed the scope to include only the victims of the 1949–54 period. In addition, the language of the April Action Program cited the importance of legal norms that would guarantee minority rights, freedom of movement, travel abroad, and protection of personal and property rights.[9] That document also included a call for the reduction in the role of the Ministry of the Interior as the supervisor of investigations. Strikingly, the "2,000 Word Manifesto" challenged the people to make efforts to secure their rights through the democratic and constitutional processes.[10]

The fourth area of reforms concerned ethnic rights and federal relations. One significant feature of this part of the reform process in Czechoslovakia impacted the formal political relations among the ethnic groups within the country. The new federal law that went into effect in 1969 was the only reform to survive the invasion. This law did establish some additional basic rights for the Slovaks who constituted roughly one-third of the population. For example, the law changed the Chamber of Nations, one of the two houses within the new national legislature, the Federal Assembly, in such a way that Czechs and Slovaks played a co-equal role. Each could select 150 representatives to the body.[11] In addition, an emphasis placed more Slovaks in administrative positions within the federal bureaucracy. In fact, the new First Secretary of the Communist party Gustav Husák went further. He appointed higher proportions of fellow Slovaks to the Presidium, the executive body of the party, as well as to the Central Committee of the Communist Party of Czechoslovakia. Although these changes heartened the Slovaks, they did not result in significantly more responsive policies. Such an improvement could only come about with more thorough transformation of the party apparatus itself.

Most observers also perceived the Czechoslovak reforms to be unusual for the bloc in that particular time period. The reform proposals themselves, in part, related to other signs of protest within East Central Europe. The plans for incorporation of a limited profit principle and price incentives paralleled those adopted in East Germany at the beginning of the 1960s. Some of the political goals connected to democratization bore the marks of the Hungarian Freedom Fighters of 1956. However, in the main, the Prague Spring of 1968 became an isolated occurrence at that point in time within the bloc. East Central European leaders such as Walter Ulbricht in East Germany and Władisław Gomułka in Poland grew very suspicious of the changes, and feared they might infect their own countries. The outcome of the crisis resulted in an invasion by the Warsaw Treaty Organization (WTO); the only time during the Cold War that this regional association took such an action against one of its own members. Tito of Yugoslavia, although not part of the WTO, sympathized with the reformers, and the Romanian leadership refused to take part in the Warsaw Pact invasion. However, in 1968, neither of those countries stood up to the rest of the bloc in any meaningful way.

Western reactions to the Warsaw Pact invasion remained muted, reactive, and unplanned. No doubt, the new foreign policy of *Ostpolitik* in West Germany had some impact on the Prague Spring reformers. Foreign Minister, and later Chancellor, Willy Brandt anchored West German foreign policy on new ties with some of the communist regimes to the east. Brandt increasingly targeted East Germany for this policy, and visits took place. Although the relationship with the Czechoslovak leadership never developed that fully, clearly the prospects tantalized the Prague Spring reformers. Possibilities for increased trade and visits across Cold War barriers may have encouraged especially the economic reformers within Czechoslovakia to continue to press their campaign to begin rolling back central controls of the economy.

On the other hand, the West stayed quite passive when the invasion by WTO forces actually took place. American President Lyndon B. Johnson denounced the move, and other Western leaders made similar statements. However, they undertook no coordinated policy to undo the invasion through active diplomacy in the United Nations or sanctions of other kinds. With respect to American ability to respond, the timing of the invasion was fortunate from the Soviet standpoint. The Johnson Administration preoccupied itself with the battle in and over Vietnam, while the presidential race to succeed Johnson reached white heat.

In sum, the unique features of the Prague Spring period are relatively clear. It was unusual for the Czechs and Slovaks to register a challenge to Soviet authority, for they had not done so in the previous twenty years. In addition, the reforms themselves included political, economic, legal/constitutional, and ethnic/federal components. Further, by 1968, most of the rest of the bloc remained relatively passive, and the outburst of reform within Czechoslovakia came as a surprise. Finally, Western reactions to the crisis did not result in any significant assistance to the Czechoslovak reformers.

Methodology

The application of content analysis covers three newspapers: the *New York Times*, the *Wall Street Journal*, and the *Christian Science Monitor*. Taken together, these papers provide a broad overview of national perspectives on the rapidly changing Czechoslovak political scene in 1968. An amount of quantitative findings emerge from such an examination. First, it is useful to look at the number of articles overall. These data will provide a glimpse of the relative importance placed on each media source on the events in Czechoslovakia. Of course, the number of columns will also reveal the general significance placed by each news source on international events overall. Second, it is useful to look at the number and percent of pieces that begin on page one. Highlighting the events in East Central Europe by positioning the essays about them on page one will be another indicator of their relative visibility. Third, insights emerge by looking at the month-by-month break down of page one columns for each newspaper. It would be expected that each newspaper would tend to cluster most articles in the summer months, when so much happened prior to the Warsaw Pact invasion. However, it may be more interesting to examine whether any news source placed importance on the reforms announced in the early months or in the impact of the invasion in the last months of the year. Table 1 and Table 2 include these data. The data for each paper are found in its index.

Table 1. Number of Articles Overall During the Prague Spring and
Page One Priority by Newspaper, 1968

Newspaper	No. of Articles	No. & Percentage of Page One Articles
N.Y. Times	1224 (approx.)[12]	215 (17.6%)
W.S. Journal	74	50 (67.6%)
C.S. Monitor	305	61 (20.0%)

From the above table the *New York Times* presented by far the
highest number of pieces on the Prague Spring and related topics. The
Christian Science Monitor contained about one quarter of the number
of articles in the *New York Times*, while the *Wall Street Journal* had
far fewer. On the other hand, the *Wall Street Journal* placed nearly
two-thirds of its columns on the front page. When its editors chose to
present information about the reform movement, they gave it full play
in the publication. The other two newspapers devoted about the same
proportion of front-page space to the series of events.

Table 2. Monthly Break-down of Articles by Newspaper
(Number Beginning on Page One), 1968

Newspaper	J	F	M	AP	MY	JN	JL	AU	S	O	N	D
N.Y. Times	1	0	10	2	19	3	31	58	45	20	19	7
W.S. Journal	0	0	0	1	1	0	11	17	11	6	2	1
C.S. Monitor	0	1	3	0	1	1	14	18	14	5	2	2

All three news sources reveal similar patterns when the examination focuses on the month of coverage. A moderate number of articles

appeared from March through May, the months when the leadership began enacting many of the key reforms. The amount of columns became heavy in July at the point when the Soviet issued serious warnings to the Czechoslovaks. A very high number of stories came out in August and September which included the period of the actual invasion and all the related reactions and developments after that fact. October compared to July as the peak period of the crisis had passed. However, numerous interpretive articles appeared in an effort to provide a broader framework for readers. Clearly the newspaper media in the United States found the drama of confrontation the most newsworthy story of the year. It may have devoted less space early in the year in the belief that the reforms seemed either not that meaningful or would not be likely to go that far.

Qualitative Findings

Analysis will focus on interpretation of key themes stressed by the newspaper media sources on a month-by-month basis throughout the year of the Prague Spring. Conclusions will be based on content analysis of topics that emerged only in columns beginning on the first page of the newspapers. These themes include the role of leadership, the reforms associated with the Prague Spring, the actual invasion by the forces of the Warsaw Treaty Organization, and Western reaction to that invasion as shown in Table 3. A final section will draw implications about the subjects that dominated the media focus in the critical year of 1968.

Table 3. Coverage of Key Themes by Newspaper
(Number & Percentage), 1968.

Newspaper	Leadership	Reforms	Invasion	Reaction	Total
N.Y. Times	37 (17.3)	36 (16.8)	99 (46.3)	42 (19.6)	214 (100)
W.S. Journal	8 (16.3)	1 (2.0)	32 (65.3)	8 (16.3)	49 (99.9)
C.S. Monitor	10 (16.4)	14 (23.0)	36 (59.0)	1 (1.6)	61 (100)

(Key Themes)

The *New York Times* provided the most balanced coverage with respect to all four themes. Each of the four subjects received a respectable amount of treatment. In contrast, the *Wall Street Journal* gave limited coverage to the reforms themselves but devoted nearly two-thirds of its reporting to the invasion. The *Christian Science Monitor* paid very little attention to the outside reaction to the Prague Spring but gave nearly three-fifths of its space to the invasion. When concentrating on the themes themselves, it is clear the topic of most interest to all editorial staffs focused on the invasion. This had become a spectacular event that conjured up all the images and stereotypes of the Cold War. At the same time, it is not surprising that coverage of the invasion overwhelmed commentary on the leadership issue and the reaction by the outside world. However, it is amazing that the reforms themselves received such a small amount of reporting early in the year. The only exception, the *Christian Science Monitor*, devoted nearly one quarter of its page one stories throughout the year to the changes enacted by the Prague Spring reformers. Perhaps the press did not expect the reforms to develop to the extent that they did or to be so consequential as to provoke the Warsaw Pact invasion.

January through March
During the first three months of 1968, the dominant themes of the leadership situation and the nature of the reforms themselves received press attention. The replacement of Novotný by Dubček in January as First Secretary of the Communist party did merit notice by the editors of the *New York Times*.[13] It proved additionally noteworthy since he became the first Slovak to head the Czechoslovak state. Conservative forces rallied around Novotný, and continued to try to keep him near the center of power. One individual attempting to fight a rearguard action against the reforms committed suicide, while another, General Jan Šejma, fled to the United States after a similar effort. Dubček dismissed two cabinet members in March, after they failed to move quickly enough in rehabilitating victims of Stalinist purges in Czechoslovakia. Novotný lost his final position as president of the republic in the same month, and the newspaper media interpreted the selection of replacement General Ludvík Svoboda, a moderate, as an effort to calm down the leadership in the Soviet Union.

The news sources placed a similar weight on the earliest reforms to be enacted by the new leadership. They noted the involvement in the reforms of Czechoslovak intellectuals and students. The anticipated impact of the reforms would be a lessened emphasis on ideology, increased autonomy from the Soviet Union, and a more independent policy towards West Germany. At the same time, the reform leadership obviously kept an eye on potential reactions by the Soviet leadership to these early changes and new themes. In late March, Dubček and Prime Minister Jozef Lenárt met with Soviet and other bloc leaders in an effort to allay their concerns, resulting in the publication by the Warsaw Pact of the Dresden Communiqué[14] causing heightened concern. Although media coverage of these early months was relatively small, readers could see a prophecy of most of the key points of tension that would inflate in ensuing months.

April through June

A small number of articles focused on the nature of the unfolding reform process. For example, in April, the *Wall Street Journal* noted that the new regime was gradually loosening state control over industry.[15] Approval of the reforms by audiences within the communist bloc merited additional commentary. Also, some Western interest arose in requests by students to reexamine the death of Foreign Minister Jan Masaryk in 1948. The applause of Tito and other Yugoslav leaders for the changes constituted one important story, and high support by a Czechoslovak public opinion poll for the effort to create a multi-party system comprised another. A vital additional voice came from American support for the reform efforts.

However, the main press interest in this period concentrated on the Soviet reaction and the implications for the Cold War. The topics of several important stories covered Soviet troop movements in Poland and in East Germany along the Czechoslovak border. Also a significant part of the chain reaction of events became assaults on the reforms. It was obvious that a number of newspapers within the bloc attacked the Prague Spring reforms. Equally important, the Soviet press reported an ideologist chastising the basic direction of the reforms. Additional criticisms took place against the memory of Thomas G. Masaryk, founder and first president of the interwar Czechoslovak experiment in democracy. Czechoslovak leaders embarked upon a series of hastily called meetings with Soviet leaders. Dubček himself flew to Moscow to describe more fully the developments taking place. President Svoboda defended the reforms in the presence of a twelve-person Soviet military delegation, and Soviet Premier Alexei Kosygin came to Prague with no advance notice. On the other hand, Kosygin's official comments seemed to be somewhat understanding of the changes in the process of being enacted. Finally, considerable Soviet pressure forced the Czechoslovak leadership to agree that Warsaw Pact maneuvers could take place in their country in the month of June. While the heavy emphasis by the Western press on the bloc reaction was understandable in light of Cold War politics, the very limited discussions of the reforms themselves proved a disservice to readers attempting to come to terms with the new dynamic of change in East Central Europe.

July through September
Heavy attention by the Western media took place during the critical months of late summer and early fall. Since each month took on a personality of its own, it makes most sense to look at the three months one-by-one.

JULY: BUILD-UP TO INVASION
The number of newspaper articles dealing with the leadership situation in Czechoslovakia and with the reforms remained relatively small. Press portrayals of Dubček presented him in a defensive light, particularly in the last weeks of the month. Under pressure from Moscow, Dubček managed to get an informal vote of confidence from resolutions passed by Czech and Slovak workers and young people meeting in cafes. In mid-July, the *New York Times* reported that conservative Central Committee members in Czechoslovakia voted their confidence in the leader.[16] However, by the end of the month, Dubček needed to deal with popular concern about an increasingly divided Communist party. Thus, he spoke to the population in order to foster a sense of stability. Increasingly, he had to communicate a sense of firmness.

Since the reforms had mainly been articulated earlier in the April Action Program,[17] the lack of attention to the changes by the newspaper media was somewhat understandable. Some of the non-Czech minorities continued to press their claims, and the Dubček leadership remained steadfastly committed to the enacted and planned modifications. External support for the reform course continued to stream in from expected sources. Tito asked for a meeting with the Czechoslovak leadership in Prague, and the League of Communists of Yugoslavia (the communist party) sent a declaration of support for the reformers. Soviet dissident Andrei Sakharov praised the Prague Spring reforms not only as bold, but also as a politically astute compromise. Thus, commitment to the path of reform rather than articulation of new ideas constituted the essence of Western press perceptions.

Preoccupation with the Soviet and Warsaw Pact reaction to the internal changes in Czechoslovakia mainly characterized the interests of the West. The *Wall Street Journal* particularly concentrated on the military maneuvers that had an obvious connection to the Czechoslovak reforms.[18] After completion of the Warsaw Pact exercises, Soviet troops withdrew very slowly from the territory of the Czechoslovak state. At the end of the month, the Soviet leaders announced new maneuvers that would take place very close to the Czechoslovak border. In this atmosphere, Czechoslovak and Soviet leaders met in eastern Slovakia in Čierna nad Tisou, with the talks very apparently filled with tension. The *Christian Science Monitor* depicted the relationship between the two nations as a drama or game in which each side sought the most advantage. It portrayed Moscow as continuously stepping up the "pressure," while the Dubček leadership constantly endeavored to "parry" new Soviet thrusts. While the Soviet leaders were "setting harsh terms," the Czechoslovak leaders tried to "hold the line" and "stand firm."[19]

The *New York Times* provided the most detailed coverage of the critical events of this build-up month. Early in July, the Prague leadership resisted Soviet efforts to get them to join in all-Warsaw Pact meetings. Fearing isolation in this kind of setting, the reformers insisted on bilateral meetings with their Soviet counterparts. In spite of their insistence, the Warsaw Pact countries met in Warsaw without the Czechoslovak leaders. Following the conclusion of the meeting, the Warsaw Treaty Organization sent a "letter" sternly warning the Czechoslovaks. In one response to that letter, Czechoslovak General Václav Prchlík stated that the WTO treaty was not intended to be used against a member state. In the middle of the month, the Johnson Administration called for negotiations between the Soviet Politburo and the Czechoslovak Presidium. Finally, the Soviet leaders pushed for such a meeting in the Soviet Union. The Czechoslovak leaders refused that setting, and finally convinced the Soviet leaders to come to Čierna. In fact, the entire eleven-person Soviet Politburo made the trip. In return for this Soviet concession, the Prague Spring leadership agreed to remove General Prchlík from the Czechoslovak Presidium. While this newspaper media portrayal certainly granted the central role to Soviet pressure, it also demonstrated that Prague could engage in a limited kind of bargaining game with Moscow.

AUGUST: THE MONTH OF INVASION

All three sources, of course, related the circumstances surrounding the August 21 invasion. The *Wall Street Journal* editors chose to touch only lightly on the facts of the invasion. That newspaper described the final efforts at dialogue between Czechoslovakia and the Soviet Union, the supportive visit to Prague of Yugoslavia's Tito, and the invasion by Warsaw Pact troops. After the invasion, the paper referenced citizen demonstrations in Czechoslovakia, as well as commenting on the Czechoslovak-Soviet talks in Moscow. However, this news source strongly emphasized the Western reaction to the invasion. In the editors' view the invasion intensified the Cold War with possible repercussions both in Southeast Asia and in the area of East-West trade. While President Johnson and Secretary of State Dean Rusk both gave ominous warnings about the damaging results of the invasion, the American public had no interest in another heavy national security commitment at a time when paralysis existed in the war in Vietnam. The *Wall Street Journal* presented only a few small references to the plight of the Czechoslovak leaders.[20]

The reporting of the *Christian Science Monitor* took on a somber tone. Some of the descriptions of the events resembled the World War Two era rather than the middle Cold War period. For instance, the day after the invasion a writer labeled the invading army as representatives of "Soviet jackboots."[21] An eyewitness concluded that "tanks shatter dreams."[22] One piece portrayed Prague as a "capital of tragedy."[23] There were, in addition, costs to the Soviet Union including a setback in relations with the West, a split among the communist parties of the world, and the emergence of hard new questions.[24]

Of course, the pages of the *New York Times* contained the most detailed coverage of the events of this critical month. Early in the month, the newspaper made an effort to interpret the result of the Čierna meetings between the leaders of the two countries. In general, the account of the final communiqué was quite positive. It appeared as though the Soviet leaders had granted concessions in such a way that the Czechoslovak leadership obtained a bit more room to maneuver. Subsequent meetings in Bratislava raised hopes even further. Those talks included other members of the WTO, and one seemingly significant outcome resulted in a reduction in the critical rhetoric emanating from both Moscow and East Berlin. Also, a discussion of splits within the Soviet leadership took place. Perhaps the diplomatic tenor of the Čierna and Bratislava meetings revealed a temporary victory by moderates over the hard-liners. Increasingly, neighboring countries began to take sides on the key issues. West German leaders became responsive to the prospects of increased trade with Czechoslovakia. They expressed a willingness to declare the 1938 Munich Pact defunct in order to ease the path in economic relations. Leaders from both Yugoslavia and Romania came to Prague to lend their support. Ulbricht in East Germany became more worried about the overtures from West Germany, and he came to the Czech spa of Karlovy Vary to try to get the Czechoslovaks to reverse course.[25]

After the middle of the month, hard-line polemics from Moscow heated up through warnings in *Pravda,* the organ of the Central Committee of the Communist Party of the Soviet Union. Following the invasion, the *New York Times* reported in detailed fashion on the critical audience in the outside world. It included in its pages individual articles on criticism from Romania, Tito, Red China, the United Nations, President Johnson, and even the Democratic Party Platform Committee in the United States.

The key follow-up event was the meeting in Moscow among all of the important WTO countries. Gomułka of Poland, Todor Zhivkov of Bulgaria, János Kádár of Hungary, and Ulbricht of East Germany met with both the Soviet and Czechoslovak leaders in a highly tense atmosphere. The final communiqué emphasized the new strategy of "normalization" meaning a return to the pre-1968 days in Czechoslovakia. While Soviet propaganda and self-justification continued, Czechoslovak leaders became mired in the position of trying to explain what they had just approved to their own population.[26]

In conclusion, it is possible to delineate somewhat different approaches to the invasion by the three newspapers. While the *Christian Science Monitor* presented the events as stark reminders of World War Two repression and totalitarianism, the *Wall Street Journal* writers tended to be somewhat optimistic early in the month about a positive outcome. The latter newspaper also emphasized both the impact on and the reactions by the outside world. Not surprisingly, trade relations remained a concern to that particular newspaper. It is difficult to characterize the approach taken by the *New York Times*. In part, it tried to communicate accurately to its readers the overall parade of events. At the same time, this news source offered a particularly useful service of keying in on splits within the Soviet leadership as a partial cause of the wavering signals coming from Moscow. It also displayed clearly the manner in which this crisis set nations in the neighborhood against one another. Finally, the newspaper recognized the plight of the Czechoslovak leadership in relations with its own population following the post-invasion Moscow meeting. In a word, the writers and editors were attuned to the domestic and international political ramifications of the crisis.

SEPTEMBER: IMMEDIATE AFTERMATH OF INVASION
The pages of the *Wall Street Journal* concentrated on a double focus on the futile efforts of the Czechoslovak leaders to mollify the Soviet leaders and on the cementing of the occupation. First, the resignation of Ota Šik was significant, for he had been the architect of the economic reforms during the middle and late 1960s. Czechoslovak leaders then held a series of meetings to talk over strategies that might lead to the end of the occupation. In addition, discussions took place over the nature of speeches given or permitted under the new circumstances. On at least one occasion, Dubček toned down a speech that might have offended the Soviet leaders.[27]

Additional steps to solidify the occupation also took place during the month. In line with Soviet expectations, Czechoslovak leaders imposed a much stricter press censorship. Officials also signed a document that linked more firmly the Czechoslovak and Soviet economies. Pressure from Moscow led to the resignation of reform-minded Foreign Minister Jiří Hayek, while other Soviet statements pressed the Czechoslovaks to speed up the process of weakening the reform forces. At the same time, the Soviets still permitted a small amount of flexibility to the Czechs and Slovaks. A certain portion of the Soviet troops pulled out of Czechoslovak cities, and the Czechoslovak press defended an official who had been ousted during the invasion. However, these concessions were clearly only possible in the period of flux that preceded "normalization."

The *Christian Science Monitor* took an interest in leadership changes within the country by publishing individual columns on the shape of the new team, the initial personnel changes in the Presidium, and the increasing pressures on the top leaders. With respect to the aftermath of invasion, the publication took a rather low-key approach. It noted both that the resistance had died down and that Prague had returned to outward normalcy. A number of other articles took the form of a summing up of the whole experience. One focused on "history's lessons," while another attempted to "tally" the "invasion score."[28] Such a muted tone offered a contrast to the dramatic and ponderous nature of pieces printed during the previous month.

Again, the *New York Times* offered the most detailed look at the unfolding events of the month. It paid relatively little attention to the leadership changes, and, none at all to the reforms that had prompted the invasion. Substantial interest in the process of consolidation with discussions between Soviet and Czechoslovak leaders formed the nub of this process for the *New York Times*. Soviet deputy Foreign Minister Vasili V. Kuznetsov met in a confrontational way in Prague with Czechoslovak President Svoboda. Both sets of leaders talked about the fourteen points that made up the essence of the Soviet demands. The Soviet leadership then sent a number of advisers with their families to Prague to assist in the setting up of the new conditions. In light of the split apparent in the communist camp during the year of the Prague Spring, Moscow called for a stronger Warsaw Pact. However, there still lingered some uncertainty in the Soviet approach during this first post-invasion month. There still remained supposedly frustration that the Czechoslovaks had not issued a clear call for help during the first half of the year. The Soviet leadership planned a big meeting in Moscow, but postponed it after disagreement emerged. Finally, the Soviets debated whether it might be wise to delay the World Communist Conference until the dust had settled a bit more.[29]

Ample attention focused as well on the Western reaction to the heavy-handed invasion. American leaders worried further about the future intensification of the Cold War. Some voices within the United States feared a set-back to arms control efforts. President Johnson thought that there no longer existed any hope for bilateral talks between America and the Soviet Union. Congress expressed concern about the jeopardy to the Nuclear Non-Proliferation Treaty, and Democratic presidential candidate Hubert H. Humphrey concluded that the invasion made a new round of arms control negotiations mandatory. A number of comments focused on new danger to the Western military alliance NATO. Secretary of Defense Clark Clifford called for greater vigilance and protectiveness of West Europe. American leaders also began to push for concrete steps that would strengthen NATO. Other international leaders, such as Secretary General of the United Nations U Thant and French President Charles De Gaulle, expressed concern about the impact of the August events on prospects for détente. The heavy emphasis by this news source on the reaction of leaders and countries outside the region reflected an effort to locate the reform/invasion cycle in a broader context of ongoing international events and processes.[30]

October through December
During the last months of the year, coverage obviously slowed down as the "normalization" process settled in. Fairly heavy reporting continued in the month of October, but November and December contained few articles with little totally new or earthshaking information.

A number of stories focused on the remaining issues connected with leadership. Gradually, Alexander Dubček lost his powers, and one writer speculated that he might eventually give up his position as head of the Czechoslovak Communist party. Also a growing perception arose that the Czechoslovak leadership disagreed about the best way to cope with the reality of "normalization." For example, a number of articles in the *New York Times* focused on the role of Prime Minister Oldřich Černík, who as an individual made a serious effort to work with the Soviet conquerors. He was the leader who traveled to Moscow to sign a treaty that legalized the invasion. He also gave a stern warning to the National Assembly about the risks inherent in too many anti-Soviet outbursts. Clearly, he responded to Soviet pressure. On the other hand, Josef Smrkovský, a key reformer, retained his job through the fall. As always, Dubček played the centrist in an effort to reconcile the two camps. In the middle of December, the Soviets permitted Černík, as a reward for his compliance, to continue as prime minister of the new federative state.[31]

A few columns looked backward at the reform movement and its aspirations. End of the year writers noted that the reforms had pretty much been wiped out by the last days of 1968, but others wondered if the Czechoslovak dream might be more "durable" than that.[32]

At the end of October 1968, on the anniversary of the founding of the Czechoslovak state, the National Assembly enacted the only reform to survive the WTO invasion when it approved the new federalization law that provided more representation to the Slovak community. Following the legislative approval, the leaders met in Bratislava to sign the law. Some demonstrations continued through late October and early November. The occasions that prompted them included celebration of the memory of Thomas G. Masaryk. There also arose clashes with policy and burning of flags in Prague as a protest on the anniversary of the 1917 Bolshevik Revolution in Russia. University students in Prague and Brno occupied buildings in protest as late as the second half of November.[33]

With regard to the "normalization" process itself, the Soviet Union required that a treaty be signed to legitimize the presence of their occupying force into the indefinite future. Although troops from the partner WTO nations began the process of leaving Czechoslovakia, approximately 100,000 Soviet troops remained in the country. Soviet representatives defended the invasion in the United Nations, and tried to defuse international anxiety about the damage to the arms control process. Soviet press attacks on the Dubček government continued, and, in December, personnel from both countries met in Kiev. Interestingly, the Soviet leaders had to deal at home with a more restive dissident group. For example, one Soviet dissident was able to publish in the Czechoslovak press a letter expressing shame for the actions of his government. Within Czechoslovakia, "normalization" meant a temporary ban on visits to the West, as well as a crackdown by the National Assembly on periodicals that continued to publish reformist ideas.

The outside world had recovered from the shock of invasion but still emitted some signals of concern. Secretary of State Rusk attacked the invasion as a violation of the UN Charter as late as early October. French Foreign Minister Michel Debré accused the Soviet leadership of creating a smoke screen by talking so much about the dangers of West German foreign policy instead of dealing seriously with the consequences of the invasion. As a result, both Secretary Rusk and West German Chancellor Kurt Kiesinger made efforts to open up talks with the Soviet Union. Discussions aimed at increasing funding for NATO took on new energy and meaning. France at least temporarily buoyed up NATO by coming back within the tent. Secretary of Defense Clifford actually outlined a plan to make NATO stronger.

NATO also issued warnings intended to deter attacks on other East Central European states. Campaigning Republicans in the United States talked about considering a delay in ratification of the Nuclear Non-Proliferation Treaty. Some observers called for development of a new strategy towards the communist bloc. Others pointed out that the invasion had contributed towards a rift within the West European communist movement. Of course, a similar split had occurred among the ruling parties of East Central Europe. As might be expected, Tito stood out as the first bloc leader to push aside brusquely the new Soviet doctrine of limited sovereignty.[34]

Press Perceptions of the Significance of the Crisis

Eruption of serious reform in 1968 in Czechoslovakia surprised literally all observers of that particular country and its regime. The transfer of power from one communist leader to another in January of that year did not seem initially consequential to either internal or external audiences. A number of substantive reasons explain and underscore this surprise. During the interwar period, there had been both genuine support for the Communist party and a sense that the West had let the nation down during the Munich Crisis of 1938. Since the 1948 communist coup, Czechoslovakia had been a relatively quiescent member of the communist bloc. There had been no serious challenges to Soviet leadership from within the communist bloc in over a decade. Many Western nations focused more on the threat of Asian communism and reactions to it than on Europe. The quagmire of war in Southeast Asia bogged down the United States, which, as well, was in the midst of a bitter, divisive presidential campaign.

Press perceptions in the United States, therefore, did not encompass much information about the reforms most central to the Prague Spring. During the first half of the year, the three news sources contained literally no page one articles that presented a discussion of the key components of the April Action Program. The emergence of a plan that implied development of a multi-party system with a full range of competitive interest groups received scant attention. The few press references made to the reforms in the early months of the year underlined mainly their foreign policy implications. Potential independence from Soviet control appeared more significant than the blossoming of democracy within the country. Accompanying this lack of interest in the reforms, the entire Czechoslovak situation prior to the summer received a really low priority. Amazingly, the increased press attention to the growing crisis in the late summer did not include many pieces that sought to explore the roots of the events.

Perhaps it was easier for the press to personalize events, and this may be more true when new developments explode with force in a surprising way on the international scene. Thus, periodically, important newspaper articles dealt with the role of leadership during the year of crisis. The press presented Alexander Dubček as a leader of promise in late spring, but as a tragic figure a few months later. Meetings of key leaders in Warsaw, Čierna, and Bratislava focused on the give and take of the bargaining process. Occasionally, useful columns spotlighted leadership splits within both the Soviet Union and Czechoslovakia. A great interest in the distinction between hard-liners and reformers was apparent. On the other hand, the press made little effort to explain to their readers the political context from which these leaders had sprung. Further, even though the August invasion marked the death knell of the reform movement, a common expectation lingered until late in the year that Dubček and his chief associates would retain their positions into the indefinite future.

By April, the press clearly fastened on the Soviet reaction as the main reality and factor in the crisis. The press depicted sudden visits by Soviet leaders to Czechoslovakia as a sign of Soviet dark intentions. Correspondingly, they portrayed the Czechoslovak leadership as subject to unexpected summonses to appear before the "enforcers" in Moscow. An understandable fascination with the moves and feints of the Soviet and Warsaw Pact troops in the region lent an even graver tone to the dynamic between the two countries. Efforts to set up meetings between the two key parties as well as the meetings themselves generated great curiosity by the press. Following the invasion, press attention centered on the polemical attacks on the Czechoslovak reformers by Moscow, the presentation of concrete demands by the Soviet leadership, and the unfolding of the "normalization" process within Czechoslovakia.

Finally, the reaction of other countries became a topic of heightened concern at various points in the crisis. Leaders within the communist bloc received ample attention in the middle part of the year. Numerous articles reported the support of Tito in Yugoslavia for the reformers. At the same time, a number of references to firm Soviet allies such as East Germany and Poland appeared. Responses by

American leaders were the subject of numerous stories, and these peaked at the time of the crisis. Official reactions by President Johnson, Secretary of State Rusk, and Secretary of Defense Clifford constituted some of these. Of course, the position of the Republican party in a presidential campaign year became a topic of a certain amount of interest. Statements and positions taken by French and German leaders were also worthy of a few press references. After the conclusion of the invasion, implications for NATO moved to the center of the stage. At some points, it seemed as if NATO unified a bit more in light of the heavy-handed move by the Warsaw Pact in Czechoslovakia. A kind of answer to the surprise demonstrated by the newspaper media in the early months of 1968 returned the world to the familiar threats and themes of the Cold War at the end of the year. The invasion resulted in a kind of marker that yanked perceptions back to the familiar framework and context of the Cold War.

CHAPTER 5

AMERICAN NEWSPAPER MEDIA PORTRAYAL OF

THE 1989 ANTI-COMMUNIST REVOLUTION

James W. Peterson

Significance of the 1989 Revolution

UNLIKE 1938, 1948, and 1968, the Czechoslovak situation in 1989 resembled the circumstances in a number of other communist-ruled nations in East Central Europe at the time. The country had undergone twenty years of unchanging centralized rule by the Gustav Husák/Miloš Jakeš regime. "Normalization"[1] after the invasion by the Warsaw Treaty Organization powers had made Czechoslovakia into one of the most conservative states in East Central Europe. In particular, few changes occurred in top leadership positions during the entire twenty-year period. The Presidium and Secretariat of the Communist party remained seemingly impervious to the process of personnel change. The leadership had abandoned the experimental economic concepts connected with the Prague Spring reformer Ota Šik. Challenges presented by Charter 77, the dissident group committed to human rights in Czechoslovakia, in the 1970s met with stern resistance. However, some economic progress continued at least up until the early 1980s. Some contended that the regime had established a bargain with the population in which individuals sacrificed personal freedoms and rights and remained politically passive because of more optimistic economic prospects.[2] Some Czechs were additionally unhappy due to their perception that Slovak First Secretary of the Communist Party of Czechoslovakia Husák had provided proportionately more political positions to Slovaks than they deserved based on their share of the population. A number of other states in the region similarly were characterized by excessive centralization, leadership stagnation, economic stalemate, and budding ethnic resentments. The changes that accompanied the anti-communist revolution included transformation of the political sphere, privatization of the economy, adoption of a legal system congruent with Western democratic norms, and radical alterations in the ethnic/federal system of government.

First, political reform really began with formation of an agenda by Charter 77. While the objectives of the Chartists did not include a formal political organization or plan, the individuals connected with the movement attempted to foster an open community of people committed to the protection of civic and human rights.[3] Clearly, Mikhail Gorbachev's reforms in the Soviet Union constituted another major impetus for political change in Czechoslovakia. In 1988, for example, Gorbachev revised the official view of the Prague Spring and the Warsaw Pact invasion. This change supported more the reform plans while criticizing the invasion.[4] During the events of November 1989, the political demands became much more concrete. Civic Forum, a coalition of Czech opposition groups which later became a shadow government by mid-December, issued a proclamation that called upon all Czechoslovak leaders, who had invited the Warsaw Pact to invade in 1968, to resign. That document also requested a formal investigation of the invasion as well as the immediate release of political prisoners. By the end of November, the political agenda expanded to include the demand that the Communist party should no longer play the leading role in the country. During December, Civic Forum members gradually replaced communists as members of the Federal Assembly, the national legislature.

Second, economic changes followed soon after completion of the initial stage of the revolution. In both Slovakia and the Czech Lands of Bohemia and Moravia, the reformers established Ministries for the Administration of National Property and Privatization. Laws enacted after 1989 included statutes that ended any limits on the proportion of foreign shares in joint ventures, restituted property of the Communist party to the people, restored land which the communists had taken from the church, permitted small-scale privatization of the service sector, and allowed large-scale privatization of the larger services and factories.[5]

Third, legal/constitutional changes were also significant. At the end of 1989, the leaders of Civic Forum drafted a new constitution that carefully defined the relationship among the various branches of government. Soon, the new leaders wrote an election law for use in 1990.[6] Political compromises resulted in indirect election of the president of the republic by the Federal Assembly, provisions for the recall of legislators from their mandates, and elections by the Federal Assembly of members of the Supreme Court.[7]

The fourth area of change included the matters of ethnic relations and federalism. Preparations for the 1990 elections revealed sharp divisions between Czechs and Slovaks. An ominous sign appeared with the creation of separate political parties in the Czech and Slovak regions. Ethnic parties representing Moravian interests in the Czech sector and Hungarian interests in the Slovakia also emerged. Behind these symbolic developments lay divisive political issues. In 1990, Slovak demands led to a formal name change of the country to the Czech and Slovak Federation. In March 1991, demonstrators in Bratislava called for Slovak independence, and President Václav Havel responded with a demand for a referendum on the matter. Slovak separatists such as Vladimir Mečiar began to complain vigorously about the higher standard of living in the Czech Lands. A series of embittering events in late 1991 set the stage for decisions in 1992 that led to the break-up of the federation.[8]

The Czechoslovak revolution of 1989 became part of a region-wide phenomenon. In fact, it came in the middle of this East Central European revolutionary year. Poland was the site of the initial challenge to Soviet bloc leadership. Election results in the late summer placed a non-communist government in charge of the country. Soon thereafter, Hungarian leadership unsealed its borders with Austria causing widespread repercussions for the Hungarian political situation as well as for fraternal relationships within the bloc. In early November, the Berlin Wall opened up for the first time, and major changes took place within East Germany. At the end of that month, massive public demonstrations happened in Prague, and, in early December, the power transition quickly took place in Czechoslovakia. Change in the Balkans came soon thereafter for Romania, and in a more evolutionary way for Bulgaria, Albania, and Yugoslavia.[9] No doubt the reforms spread like a prairie fire within the region. In that sense, the Czechoslovak changes received inspiration from the process of renewal taking place in surrounding countries. Probably, the mass demonstrations, one of the unique features of the Czechoslovak revolution, had a delayed ripple effect on changes in such Balkan countries as Croatia and Bosnia in the mid-1990s.

In addition, the outcome of the reform movement in Czechoslovakia paralleled results in a number of other countries in the region. The emergence of a non-communist transitional government formed only the first step in a profound set of changes. Early in 1990, the new leaders established the democratic process in earnest. Totally free elections took place in the late spring, and the normal development of political parties and interest groups occurred. Just as the bloc nations had moved in lock-step formation on so many structural and policy features in the communist era, so they all moved toward democratic patterns in similar ways at about the same time.

The West also played an indirect, but continuous and involved role in the period directly preceding the 1989 revolution. American President Ronald Reagan, during the 1980s, had tried to develop a proactive policy that would weaken the economy and will of the Soviet Union, and the first Bush Administration gave encouragement to the reforming regimes in the second half of 1989.[10] While the Bush Administration committed itself to a renewed foreign policy in the wake of the Iran-Contra scandal, the Soviet regime wearied after nearly a decade of war in neighboring Afghanistan. As President George H. W. Bush welcomed one new post-communist government after another, he claimed some credit on behalf of the United States for the actual outcome of events.

Further, the 1989 revolutions throughout the bloc tended to have severe destabilizing effects on ethnically divided states. In nearly every case, the eruption of deeply rooted historical rivalries accompanied the casting off of communist rule. This pattern became particularly evident in Czechoslovakia when the government enacted democratic procedures. For example, separate political party structures emerged in the two parts of the country. Civic Forum, the force behind the 1989 revolution, and its spin-offs became the primary political vehicle of Czech political aspirations. In contrast, Public Against Violence, the Civic Forum's counterpart in Slovakia, initially developed into the principal engine of political desires of the Slovaks. Although Slovaks obtained more political rights in the new democratic state than they enjoyed during communist times, ominous signs pointed to the eventual break-up of 1993 into two separate nation-states: the Czech Republic and Slovakia. Certainly,

Czechs and Slovaks tried unsuccessfully in remaining together in common political parties in the aftermath of the completed revolution. Further, they developed a complicated and unworkable formula for making key political decisions, including the selection of the president of the republic. Major decisions required a three-fifths vote of support within the national legislature as well as in the two legislatures anchored in the Bohemian-Moravian and Slovak regions. These internal pressure points surrounding the fact of ethnicity paralleled the developing time bombs that threatened Yugoslavia and Romania.

In conclusion, the key themes of the 1989 revolution in Czechoslovakia reflected mirrors of similar dynamics affecting much of the rest of East Central Europe. The dimensions of their reforms included the politics, economics, the legal/constitutional arena, and the ethnic/federal dimension. The common regional dynamics included the simultaneous rebellion against unchanging communist dinosaurs, the successful post-revolutionary establishment of a chain of similar democracies, the engaged and proactive role of the West, and the consequence of unraveled ethnic relationships.

Methodology and Quantitative Findings

Content analysis used five national and four regional newspapers. The national papers included the *New York Times*, the *Wall Street Journal*, the *Christian Science Monitor*, *USA Today*, and the *Washington Post*, while the regional newspapers consisted of the *Boston Globe*, the *Chicago Tribune*, the *Atlanta Journal-Constitution*, and the *Los Angeles Times*, representing a different section of the United States. The analysis will include a brief assessment of the number of articles contained in each of the nine papers. These findings will display the relative importance placed on the events by each news source. There will also be a spotlight placed on the percentage of articles that start on page one for each newspaper. Attention to the month-by-month break down of page one columns can reveal the extent to which any paper followed the crisis from its origin to its completion. Also, data on comparative column length of articles are available for all of these news sources, for, in recent decades, indices have included such information. Basically, papers that include higher percentages of longer pieces place greater significance on the events being reported. Data for each news source were derived from its index.

Table 1. Number of Articles Overall During the Revolution and
Page One Priority by Newspaper, 1989.

Newspaper	No. of Articles	No. & Percentage of Page One Articles
New York Times (1)	186	36 (19.4)
Wall Street Journal (2)	54	33 (61.1)
Christian Science Monitor (3)	41	8 (19.5)
USA Today (4)	21	3 (14.3)
Washington Post (5)	97	25 (25.8)
Boston Globe (6)	67	14 (20.9)
Chicago Tribune (7)	71	10 (14.1)
Atlanta Journal-Constitution (8)	41	12 (29.3)
Los Angeles Times (9)	92	34 (37.0)

Data for the five national papers are quite varied. The highest number of articles appeared in the *New York Times*, but the *Wall Street Journal* placed over sixty per cent of its columns on the front page. Although the *Christian Science Monitor* had fewer pieces than either of the other two, the proportion of page one articles compared to that for the *New York Times*. Data for the two other national newspapers range divergently. *USA Today* had a small number of pieces and a tiny proportion which began on page one. On the other hand, the number of articles in the *Washington Post* was higher than the number for any other national newspaper with the obvious exception of the *New York Times*; a full quarter of those columns began on the first page.

The data for the four regional newspapers also present a picture of contrasts. In terms of number of articles and proportion on the first page, the lead went to the *Los Angeles Times*. Apparently, interest on the West Coast stayed high in these far-off European events. While the number of overall articles remained low for the *Atlanta Journal-Constitution*, the proportion that began on the first page was relatively high. Figures for the *Boston Globe* match those for the national (East Coast) publications. Finally, the *Chicago Tribune* contained a respectable number of pieces but placed very few on the front page concluding that in that part of the Midwest interest in these events appeared only moderate.

Table 2. Monthly Breakdown of Articles by Newspaper (Number Beginning on Page One).

										Month		
Newspaper	J	F	M	AP	MY	JN	JL	A	S	O	N	D
(1)	0	1	0	0	0	0	0	0	0	1	19	15
(2)	5	2	3	0	2	0	0	3	3	5	5	5
(3)	0	0	0	0	0	1	0	1	0	0	1	5
(4)	0	0	0	0	0	0	0	0	0	0	2	1
(5)	0	0	0	0	0	0	0	0	1	3	11	10
(6)	0	0	0	0	0	0	0	0	0	0	11	3
(7)	0	0	0	0	0	0	0	0	0	0	5	5
(8)	0	0	0	0	0	0	0	0	0	2	7	3
(9)	1	0	0	0	0	0	0	0	0	2	17	14

It is also useful to examine the heaviest coverage months for the nine newspapers whereas the five national news sources all placed the heaviest emphasis on Czechoslovakia at the end of the year. This was true with respect to all the articles included, as well as for page one pieces alone. For the most part, in Czechoslovakia the mass demonstrations took place in late November and the major governmental changes in early December. Thus, logically these two months entailed the heaviest reporting. Several of the national newspapers also provided some coverage in the early months of the year. For example, in the first three months of the year, the *New York Times* had one front-

page article, while the *Wall Street Journal* had ten; the regional papers
followed the same trend. Nearly all of the page one columns appeared
in the last two months of the year. In the early months of the year,
only the *Los Angeles Times* included a page one story. These findings
reinforce the conclusion that the momentous changes that occurred in
East Central Europe in the second half of the year caught the newspaper media by surprise.

Table 3. Column Length of Articles by Newspaper (Number and Percentage)

Newspaper	Short (6 in.)	Medium (6–18 in.)	Long (18+ in)	Total
(1)*	79 (42.5)	56 (30.1)	0	186 (100)
(2)	N/A	N/A	N/A	0
(3)	3 (7.3)	14 (34.1)	24 (58.5)	41 (100)
(4)	4 (19.0)	15 (71.4)	2 (9.5)	21 (100)
(5)	0	35 (36.1)	62 (63.9)	97 (100)
(6)	2 (3.0)	40 (59.7)	25 (37.3)	67 (100)
(7)	3 (4.2)	41 (57.7)	27 (38.0)	71 (100)
(8)	5 (12.2)	22 (53.6)	14 (34.1)	41 (100)
(9)	2 (2.2)	25 (27.2)	65 (70.6)	92 (100)

*For the *New York Times* there were 51 articles (27.4%) for which no column
length was listed.

A number of newspapers clearly stand out in terms of providing a
high proportion of lengthy, in-depth articles. The leader, the *Los
Angeles Times*, provided long essays in a little over seventy percent of
the cases. The *Washington Post* and *Christian Science Monitor* came in
only a little behind this pace, as both included lengthy essays in well
over half of the cases. At the other end of the spectrum, *USA Today*

included long pieces less than ten per cent of the time. When the focus switched to medium length articles, the papers which had relatively small percentages of lengthy columns partly compensated for that situation. For instance, *USA Today* contained over seventy percent of its articles in this category. The *Boston Globe*, the *Chicago Tribune*, and the *Atlanta Journal-Constitution* presented similar patterns.

Unfortunately, no data of this sort existed for the *Wall Street Journal*. It is also difficult to interpret the information from the *New York Times*. While it had the highest proportion of short articles, this daily provided to its readers nearly twice as many pieces overall as did the periodical in second place in terms of numbers of pieces. Missing data on some columns make further analysis of the *New York Times* complicated. Generally, there were no resounding patterns in these data. Two of the three national papers with complete data devoted a substantial amount of space to a high proportion of essays. Three of the four regional dailies provided moderate coverage in a high proportion of cases. Thus, a slight tendency for national papers existed to include more in-depth articles and for regional newspapers to offer moderate-length pieces that mainly provided the facts of the situation.

Qualitative Findings

Key themes emerged during the year 1989, and the newspaper media repeatedly came back to them throughout the year. The topics included the role of leadership, the protests against the old regime, the nature of the changes themselves, and the reaction of the outside world. Analysis will proceed on a month-by-month basis with a distinction made between the perceptions of the five national sources and the four regional newspapers. The final section will outline the central findings about newspaper media perceptions of the year of transformation.

The most balanced coverage of all four themes took place on the pages of the *Washington Post*. The *Wall Street Journal* did not provide much coverage of the leadership issue or of the process of democratic change, while the *New York Times* did not give much central reporting of the outside reaction to the changes. The relatively small number of page one stories for the *Christian Science Monitor* and for *USA Today* resulted in unmeaningful patterns. With respect to the subjects themselves, the *New York Times* provided the highest proportion of coverage to the leadership theme, while the *Wall Street*

Journal emphasized in numerous stories the mass protests that took place in the fall.

Table 4. Coverage of Key Themes by Newspaper (Number and Percentage), 1989.

| Newspaper | Key Themes | | | | |
	Leadership	Protests	Change	Reaction	Total
(1)	15 (41.7)	13 (36.1)	7 (19.4)	1 (2.8)	36 (100)
(2)	1 (3.0)	17 (51.5)	3 (9.1)	12 (36.4)	33 (100)
(3)	1 (12.5)	3 (37.5)	4 (50.0)	0	8 (100)
(4)	0	1 (33.3)	2 (66.7)	0	3 (100)
(5)	6 (24.0)	5 (20.0)	7 (28.0)	7 (28.0)	25 (100)
(6)	5 (35.7)	4 (28.6)	3 (21.4)	2 (14.3)	14 (100)
(7)	2 (20.0)	0	4 (40.0)	4 (40.0)	10 (100)
(8)	3 (25.0)	4 (33.3)	2 (16.7)	3 (25.0)	12 (100)
(9)	6 (18.2)	5 (15.2)	12 (36.4)	10 (30.3)	33 (100.1)

Among the regional papers, the *Los Angeles Times* offered the striking finding again with its relatively high number of page one articles. This newspaper provided relatively even coverage of each of the four topics, with the process of democratic change being the favorite. Balanced coverage of themes took place also in the *Boston Globe* and the *Atlanta Journal-Constitution*. However, the former put the heavier emphasis on leadership themes, while the latter gave the greater importance to the mass demonstrations and protests. The *Chicago Tribune* published no front page coverage of the protests, but it did present the highest proportion of columns on the outside reaction to the changes. In this situation in 1989, clearly no pattern to the coverage existed among the regional dailies. In fact, each of the four regional news sources chose to give its greatest page one emphasis to a different topic.

This outline of themes revealed principally that the coverage of the 1989 revolution did not fit any standard, cookbook formula for the nine papers studied. No sharp distinction could be found either between the reporting provided by the national or regional newspaper media. Most important, each source took its own independent approach towards selection of subjects that deserved page one emphasis.

January through March
References to events in Czechoslovakia appeared in only two national newspapers and in no regional sources. Mass protests in the country received the most attention. In fact, the *Wall Street Journal* had the greatest interest in these anti-regime activities. It described the process by which the police broke up demonstrations centering on the twentieth anniversary of the public suicide of Jan Palach, who, in 1969 had set himself on fire to protest the Soviet occupation and the end of the Prague Spring Reforms. The financial source noted the arrest of eight hundred demonstrators at one of these events.[11] This newspaper, as well as the *New York Times*, reported the efforts of the authorities to punish the playwright Václav Havel and seven others for fomenting the protests surrounding the Palach anniversary. As well, the government arrested a key spokesperson for Charter 77 for inciting one of these riots. Efforts to obtain release of the new political prisoners through circulation of a petition led to a jailing of several others.[12] A few of the articles emphasized outside reactions to these developments in Czechoslovakia. American officials criticized the country and its neighbors for human rights violations. Soviet leadership rival Yegor Ligachev visited Czechoslovakia praising its collective farm system. Some interpreted his remarks as veiled criticism for Soviet leader Mikhail Gorbachev's reforms and their implications for bloc nations.[13]

April through June
Only a handful of articles appeared in the spring months, as most Western press observers assumed that "normalization" had been reestablished. However, the *Wall Street Journal* did note that the authorities paroled Havel after he had completed only half of his sentence.[14] Despite this move by the regime, the *Christian Science Monitor* included an analysis that concluded that glasnost, the policy of "openness," had not yet made as much progress in Czechoslovakia as it had in the Soviet Union, Poland, or Hungary.[15]

July through September

A few pieces appeared in August as the anniversary of the Warsaw Pact invasion of 1968 neared. Police detained dozens of Czechoslovak citizens on the eve of the demonstrations, and then, beat a number of them at the time of the mass protests on August 21. The press continued to portray the regime as very conservative in a region beginning to sense the tremors of change. The pressure for emigration to the West increased considerably in mid-September. While Hungary decided to permit East Germans to go into the West and Poland nodded in agreement, the Husák/Jakeš regime in Czechoslovakia impassively made no comment. In fact, Czechoslovak authorities began to seize the passports of potential émigrés. As October neared, the Western press had clearly characterized Czechoslovakia throughout the year as unlikely to be caught up in changes affecting other countries in the region.

October through December

OCTOBER: BUILD-UP TO REVOLUTION

Although attention focused primarily on other East Central European countries during the month of October, the number of articles on the situation in Czechoslovakia grew. Two of the regional newspapers even gave some limited coverage to that country. Early in the month, the Western interest centered on the plight of East Germans who went to Prague in order to leave for the West. Thousands of East Germans entered the West German Embassy in Prague, and then traveled by train to West Germany. The East German regime permitted a large number of its citizens to leave in this way, but on October 4, they banned further visits to Czechoslovakia. One story described a group of refugees left behind in Dresden who subsequently fought with police forcing them to stay in East Germany.[16] Of course, the police in Czechoslovakia tried to bloc these East Germans from getting into the West German Embassy in Prague, but the number of refugees grew so large that this attempt proved fruitless. Literally, all of these columns early in the month stressed the way in which the outside world reacted to the more open travel regulations established in Czechoslovakia.

At the end of the month, mass demonstrations occurred on the anniversary of the founding of the Czechoslovak state. Protesters used this occasion as a vehicle to call for both the deposal of party leader Miloš Jakeš and the holding of free elections. Also an international human rights meeting took place at the same time in Prague. In both cases, the police crushed the demonstrations. Thus, as the month ended, the spotlight switched from Czechoslovakia's external relations with the two German states to internal demonstrations calling for a major change in the political system. As such, these events at the end of the month pointed to the enormous changes that would take place in November.

NOVEMBER: MONTH OF THE REVOLUTION

Two of the national newspapers gave fairly limited coverage to the momentous events in November. Obviously, Czechoslovakia was not the only nation in tumult. Truly, also a more dramatic story for Western audiences in early November concerned the collapse of the Berlin Wall. This event, no doubt, symbolized the end of the Cold War, and so the Czechoslovak events, coming so soon thereafter may have seemed to some both inevitable and a bit anticlimactic. However, the *Christian Science Monitor* did carry one story about the end-of-the month demonstrations, plans for a general strike, and the agenda of Civic Forum.[17] A few similar articles appeared on page one of *USA Today* which also provided some coverage to the changing composition of the government.[18]

The national news sources, the *New York Times*, the *Washington Post*, and the *Wall Street Journal* carried the most extensive reporting. In each of these papers, the main story focused on the series of mass protests that eventually felled the regime. The *New York Times* described fully the daily demonstrations, the use of force by police against the demonstrators, the role of students and professors, and the magic invoked with the appearance of Alexander Dubček, the leader of the ill-fated Prague Spring. Clearly workers played a role in these demonstrations. For example, Prague workers took part in one general strike, and read from the Declaration of Independence.[19] The *Washington Post* mentioned the same events but also linked them to the widening splits within the leadership of the Communist party. They also highlighted the role of airline employees in one of the general strikes.[20] In sum, the emphasis concentrated on the continuing nature of the demonstrations, the breadth of the opposition coalition, and their impact on the government.

Near the end of the month, the process of political change began to receive major treatment by the press. The first major concessions involved the announcement by Prime Minister Ladislav Adamec on November 22 that some non-communists could join the cabinet. At the very end of the month more substantive compromises resulted. Non-communists actually entered the government, the regime dropped the compulsory requirement of Marxism-Leninism in the schools, and Civic Forum won access to the mass media. Party leaders also abandoned the constitutional language that referred to the leading political role of the Communist party. Similarly, the legislature removed from the state charter the provision that established Marxism as the foundation of public education.

The national newspapers contained a handful of essays about the theme of leadership. Leadership references included a description of the fall of party secretary Jakeš, commentary on the rising role of caretaker Prime Minister Adamec, nostalgic references to the reemergence of Dubček, and several articles on the ouster of the hard-liners from the cabinet. Interestingly, none of these sources contained any pieces about the reaction of the outside world. The riveting internal events themselves drew all attention like a magnet.

The regional papers presented some notable differences. Readers of the *Boston Globe* would have learned the most about the leadership situation. Coverage of Dubček and the decline of the hard-liners drew most of its attention. The second most popular story for that newspaper became the protest movement, but the reforms actually enacted did not receive much coverage.[21] In contrast, the few articles in the *Chicago Tribune* put primary emphasis on the bargaining game at the top that resulted in important changes within the cabinet.[22] The *Atlanta Journal-Constitution* differed from the other two by focusing on the mass demonstrations. They had four essays on the protests, but only one on each of the other three themes.[23] Finally, the *Los Angeles Times* distinguished itself through its inclusion of the highest number of page one articles among the regional newspapers. The West coast journal gave a representative amount of coverage to all four topics but concentrated on the regime changes. It described the key personnel shifts, but reserved the greatest emphasis for the role of the opposition. This reporting included individual columns on the history of anti-regime groups, the organizational skills of Civic Forum, and the increasing role of television in the opposition movement.[24] Clearly, each of the regional newspapers placed its own special imprint on the perception and interpretation of those far-away events.

DECEMBER: AFTERMATH OF THE REVOLUTION

Coverage by the national newspapers remained quite heavy in the month of December. As the need for protests and demonstrations disappeared, however, the focus switched to the process of making the transition from communist authoritarianism to democratic patterns. The *Christian Science Monitor* called attention to the efforts of a divided Civic Forum to form a coalition government.[25] The *Wall Street Journal* took an interest in specific steps such as the opening of the border with Austria and the repeal of laws that punished dissidents.[26] The main thrust of *Washington Post* articles reported on the actual governmental alterations that were taking place including personnel changes in the cabinet, the agreement of the Communist party to play a minority role, the swearing in of the new government, and the introduction of town meetings in certain Czechoslovak municipalities.[27]

Nearly equal in importance was the focus placed by these newspaper media on the role of political leadership. Marian Čalfa replaced Adamec as prime minister leading to an agreement to a cabinet filled by a majority of non-communists, an event coordinated with the resignation of Gustav Husák as president. Near the end of the month, heightened interest appeared in both the rise of new leaders and division of offices among them. Václav Havel bargained with the Communist party over the nature of electing the next president. His proposal for election by the legislature won out over the latter's suggestion of direct popular election. Havel and Dubček ended up splitting two of the key offices. While the legislature elected Dubček as its chair on December 29, the same body chose Havel as president the next day. The election of Havel had been coordinated as well with the resignation of Jakeš as head of the Communist party.

Only a handful of articles reported on protests. At the beginning of the month, demonstrations by 150,000 persons in part led to the emergence of the first non-communist cabinet. Toward the middle of the month, a major celebratory demonstration on the anniversary of a key march occurred on the same date in the previous month. Coverage of reactions by the outside world remained equally slim. The only major event worth noting became the joint decision by the Soviet Union and the Warsaw Pact to invalidate their 1968 invasion of Czechoslovakia. Perhaps the small number of pieces on global reactions resulted due to the fact that the public had been observing dramatic changes in nearly all countries of the region for a number of months.

The regional news sources also divided their articles between the changing leadership patterns and the rapid series of major governmental transformations. Noteworthy, the *Los Angeles Times* took the greatest interest in the December events in Czechoslovakia. It covered most of the events that the national newspapers had mentioned. However, it had a unique interest in the military and defense implications of the political changes perhaps due to the impact the fall of communism would have on the large number of defense contractors on the West Coast. Several essays included commentary on the reinterpretation of the 1968 Warsaw Pact invasion. It also included important articles on the announced plan for removal of the Soviet troops, the voiced intentions to reduce the size of the Czechoslovak army, and the plan to take down the fence on the West German border. Other changes such as the initial steps to dismantle state control of the economy also caught its attention.[28] The paper's coverage of such matters was more extensive than that provided by the national news sources.

Press Perceptions of the Significance of the Crisis

Several impressions shine through the newspaper media coverage of the actual anti-communist revolution of 1989. The priority which sources placed on the Czechoslovak chapter of that revolutionary year varied from paper to paper. The *New York Times* paid much attention to the changes, while *USA Today* provided little coverage. In addition, heavy reporting was not confined to the East Coast-based national newspapers. For example, the *Los Angeles Times* included a relatively high proportion of page one stories about the political transformation of Czechoslovakia. On the other hand, the *Chicago Tribune* devoted very little space to the story. Thus, varied coverage existed among the regional papers as well as among the national news sources. Also, no central theme elicited the most newspaper media interest. Some sources showed more interest in the mass protests, while others gave fairly detailed analysis and consistent coverage to the establishment of democratic processes. As the Cold War ended, no main picture appeared like the Warsaw Pact invasion of 1968 that helped the newspaper media organize perceptions. This reality freed the news sources to treat the changes of 1989 in very individual ways.

At the same time, there continued one underlying theme in press perceptions of the 1989 revolution relating to the fact that the changes in Czechoslovakia came in the midst of a season of transformation in

East Central Europe. Major changes occurred earlier in the year in Poland, Hungary, and East Germany. Calls for a new direction began to take place in the Balkans as well. In fact, only the Czechoslovak and Romanian regimes had not yet made any concessions to the opposition forces. Therefore, the unfolding events in Czechoslovakia seemed unsurprising and almost expected. This may help explain why the press coverage possessed the features it did.

The leadership theme received a proportionate share of attention, but many of the figures had familiar faces: Václav Havel, the well-known playwright and dissident, and Alexander Dubček, who had penetrated the Western consciousness through his catalytic role in 1968. Their central roles in the new government did not come as a surprise. By the same token, to careful observers of East Central Europe, Gustav Husák was reasonably familiar, while Miloš Jakeš was not. Jakeš's reputation as an unyielding hard-liner made it easy for readers in the United States to place him in a classification with other communist-era dinosaurs.

Of course, much press attention concentrated on the mass demonstrations. Early in the year, these protests centered on the incarceration of Václav Havel, but at the end of the year, they became the forum in which the new demands emerged. They also constituted the fulcrum of opposition that eventually dislodged the regime. However, the press portrayals of these mass protests contained a sense of inevitability. No article voiced astonishment that the Czechoslovak communist regime failed either to prevent or to repress them. After following the process by which East German citizens first found alternative means for leaving their country and later discovered that they could even cross over the Berlin Wall, Western readers prepared themselves to understand why this exercise in democratic freedoms could take place in that type of system.

The press even treated the subject of the process of change in a low-key manner. Newspaper discussions of the rise of a cabinet with a non-communist majority never questioned whether such a development would take place. The articles simply contained the implicit question of when that event would come to pass. Similarly, the sources interpreted the passing of the torch from Jakeš and Husák to Havel as a relatively routine event. So many communist leaders had given way to opposition figures during the last few months within East Central Europe. Discussion of elections in Czechoslovakia, along with reactivation of moribund domestic political institutions, seemed almost to be the expected, ordinary course of events. They contained no genuine surprise.

Finally, the paucity of press coverage of the last theme of reactions outside the country is worthy of mention. Significant response arose in the West to both the election of a non-communist government in Poland much earlier in the year, and, later, the fall of the Berlin Wall. Despite the power of the daily mass demonstrations in Czechoslovakia, these protests, in a sense, seemed only another act in a play that the West had been applauding all year. Ironically, the principal outside replies came from the Soviet Union. Soviet leaders felt impelled to apologize for past violations of Czechoslovakia's freedom, and this demonstrated the extent to which they had bought into the process of more freedom for former bloc partners. Had the Czechoslovak events in 1989 been isolated ones as in 1938, 1948 and 1968, then they might have created more of a stir in the West. In fact, the changes in Czechoslovakia resulted in a major surprise when contrasted with the political situation the nation found itself even one year earlier, but they were unsurprising when caught in the midst of a series of similar events within the neighborhood.

CHAPTER 6

CARICATURING CZECHOSLOVAKIA IN

AMERICAN POLITCAL CARTOONS[1]

Gregory C. Ference & A. Paul Kubricht

OLITICAL CARTOONS have a long history in the United States
first appearing before the American Revolution largely to par-
ody British policies in the colonies. From this time, these
drawings became a mainstay of American political commen-
tary. Cartoonists distill events and political issues using pictures and a
minimum of words by employing various means including carica-
tures, exaggerations, symbolism, satire, and irony. Usually found on
editorial pages of newspapers, these representations make the readers
think about current issues, but also provide historians with insight
into the spirit and biases of the time.

Political cartoonists portrayed the events, issues, and personalities
during the crises Czechoslovakia faced in the twentieth century.
These caricaturists captured the images and molded perceptions of
Czechoslovakia seen by the broader reading public in the events of
1938, 1948, and 1968. By 1989, the cartoonists presented Czechoslovakia as part of a broader movement toward democratization in East
Central Europe without emphasizing its individual role in the events
during the collapse of communism.

1938: The Munich Crisis

Czechoslovakia faced its first major international crisis in the late
summer and early fall 1938. Adolf Hitler, the aggressive, land-hungry
Nazi dictator of Germany, challenged the territorial integrity and
national sovereignty of the small, independent, democratic country.

HOW JOHN BULL MAKES A SACRIFICE

Figure 1
HOW JOHN BULL MAKES A SACRIFICE
New York Post, 8 September 1938.

In Figure 1, the octopus, representing Nazi Germany, clutches the leg, symbolizing the region of the Sudetenland, of the sailor Czechoslovakia. Rather than easily resorting to shooting the Nazi sea monster with his readily available rifle thereby ending the threat, England, the master of the seas represented by John Bull, employs "appeasement" by willingly sawing off the point of confrontation of his fellow democracy Czechoslovakia. This prophetic political cartoon foretold British unwillingness to oppose Nazi aggression by force, and cleverly portrays the final result of the Munich Agreement.

Despite the numerous concessions offered by the Czechoslovak government to the Sudeten Germans, including the "Fourth Plan" granting virtually all their demands, German Chancellor Hitler labeled these proposals as insufficient and his patience was wearing thin. Figure 2 shows that the Sudeten Germans no longer mattered in the crisis, but rather it was the aggressive Hitler who was manipulating them. He would not be placated by Czechoslovak concessions by arrogantly turning his back on them. Instead, somehow the fault rested with Czechoslovakia for the controversy.

In Figure 3, the ancient writer of events, or the Muse of "History," smiles approvingly as he records for the future record one of the significant events of 1938, indicating that British Prime Minister Neville Chamberlain had broken all precedents by using modern technology to fly to meet Hitler in an attempt to preserve peace in Europe and resolve the crisis. In such a tense and heated international atmosphere, the only hope for Czechoslovakia remained the vindication of history.

In Figure 4, the *Chicago Tribune* interestingly parodied the Munich Agreement by attempting to introduce a new word into the English language: "Czechoslovaked" meaning that one has been being mercilessly run over by an automobile or "sucker punched." After being thrashed soundly or "Czechoslovaked" in the National League baseball pennant race of 1938 by the Chicago Cubs, the Pittsburgh Pirates commiserate with the Czechoslovaks who have just been throttled by four European powers.

With the signing of the Munich Agreement, the world relaxed as peace seemed assured. Figure 5 shows both sides exhibiting great relief after the meeting. British Prime Minister Chamberlain, with his trademark umbrella, and his ally, French Premier Edouard Daladier, quickly leave Munich expressing relief in adverting war by wiping their brows with the public in the background sharing such feeling.

"My Patience Is Near The End"

Figure 2
"My Patience Is Near The End"
The Baltimore Sun, 9 September 1938
© 1938, reprinted with the permission of *The Baltimore Sun*.

The Old Scribe Goes Modern

Figure 3
The Old Scribe Goes Modern
The Baltimore Sun, 16 September 1938
© 1938, reprinted with the permission of *The Baltimore Sun*.

Figure 4
CZECHOSLOVAKED!
Chicago Tribune, 1 October 1938
Copyrighted with Permission KRT/Tribune Media Services.

'Whew! That Was A Close Call!'

Figure 5
Whew! That Was A Close Call!
The Salisbury Times (MD), 3 October 1938
Copyright *Herblock: A Cartoonist's Life* (Times Books, 1998).

Hitler, himself relieved after publicly taking a belligerent stance against Czechoslovakia and the Western allies throughout the September crisis and having secured his demands at Munich, also wipes his brow. Yet, he does so out of public view thereby demonstrating that his impregnable stance of not backing down was correct. In so doing, he sustained his image as a staunch, unyielding defender of German rights across East Central Europe.

1948: The February Revolution
Less than ten years after Munich, Czechoslovakia once more became the center of an international crisis. This time a Soviet takeover threatened Czechoslovakia's independence. Political cartoonists again depicted a situation of a larger, totalitarian country taking control of a smaller, democratic state. In 1948, Czechoslovakia would not escape the memory of 1938.

In Figure 6, Soviet leader Joseph Stalin smiles after seizing Czechoslovakia in the February coup. He confidently waits to add further "real estate" of Finland, Manchuria, and Korea to his already vast empire. He looks at a picture of his one-time ally, Adolf Hitler, who lost World War Two in his quest for world domination, and states slyly on his own successful tactics of acquiring territory, "What a Clumsy Operator You Were!"

After the Nazis held Czechoslovakia captive from 1938/1939 to 1945, the country enjoyed less than three years of democracy and independence following the Second World War. With the February coup, the country once again became a prisoner; instead of the Nazi Germans, the Soviet Russians controlled the fate of Czechoslovakia. The representation in Figure 7 shows the large ball-and-chain, symbolizing first Nazi, then Soviet domination, that little Czechoslovakia was forced to pull. This ball-and-chain of oppression remained the same, only the captor's ideology had changed.

The final "Iron Curtain" of Soviet domination and repression in Figure 8 crushes with its massive weight the independent and democratic Czechoslovakia represented in the person of President Edvard Beneš. After sitting in the audience and watching the performance of the Soviet seizure of East Central Europe, Beneš, representing the Czechoslovaks, is himself grabbed and, despite his efforts to resist, he is dragged behind the Iron Curtain to become part of the cast of Soviet-dominated Europe. A little country has once again fallen under totalitarian

Figure 6
"What a Clumsy Operator You Were!"
The Salisbury Times (MD), 6 March 1948
With permission of *The Salisbury Times.*

Postwar Changeover

Figure 7
Postwar Changeover
Chicago Tribune, 28 February 1948
Copyrighted with Permission KRT/Tribune Media Services.

One Less in the Audience—One More in the Cast

Figure 8
One Less in the Audience—One More in the Cast
Chicago Daily News, 26 February 1948
Copyright permission pending.

control, however, this time there is no Chamberlain or Western Powers to blame.

The last bright light of freedom in a dark, oppressive communist government chose suicide rather than dictatorship thereby becoming a martyr in Figure 9. The post-coup communist government of Czechoslovakia included one democrat, Jan Masaryk, who as foreign minister gave some credibility to the events of February. Masaryk, son of Czechoslovakia's founder and first president, Thomas G. Masaryk, and a proponent of his father's idea of Western democracy, was a popular figure at home and abroad.

As indicated in Figure 10, a decade separates the Munich Agreement from the February coup. During both traumatic events, the Nazis and the communists, respectively, bullied Edvard Beneš, president of Czechoslovakia, who behaved with dignity throughout each crisis. The only difference between the two experiences was the allegiance of the protesters clamoring for change. This cartoon is in much the same vein as Figure 7; the noble stand of the weak is crushed by an evil, more powerful nation.

Figure 11 shows the new communist constitution of Czechoslovakia promulgated in May 1948 banishing Edvard Beneš, who resigned the presidency in early June rather than sign it into law as demanded by the communists. As the former president leaves office he carries the lifeless body of Czechoslovak national freedom. Accompanying him are the ghosts of the builders of Czechoslovak statehood and democracy, the first president of Czechoslovakia Thomas G Masaryk and Woodrow Wilson, who as president of the United States played an important role in the birth of Czechoslovakia in 1918 and 1919. These ghosts of Czechoslovakia's democratic past escort a living Beneš while the pathos of the death of liberty again haunts Czechoslovakia.

1968: The Prague Spring

Twenty years later, in 1968, Czechoslovakia again became the center of world attention when the Prague Spring occurred. Alexander Dubček, the communist leader of Czechoslovakia, attempted to introduce "socialism with a human face," but after less than a year in power, he faced a Soviet invasion. Again the might and power of a large neighbor overwhelmed little Czechoslovakia.

Figure 12 depicts peaceful Czechoslovak picnickers enjoying the democratic liberalizing policies of the Prague Spring. They are threat-

Give Me Liberty Or Give Me Death!

Figure 9
Give Me Liberty Or Give Me Death!
San Francisco Chronicle, 11 March 1948
C.T. Sweigert/San Francisco Chronicle.

A Decade of Dignity

Figure 10
A Decade of Dignity
San Francisco Chronicle, 28 February 1948
C.T. Sweigert/*San Francisco Chronicle*.

Figure 11
"HE MOURNS THE DEAD WHO LIVES AS THEY DESIRE"
The Evening Bulletin (Philadelphia) 9 June 1948
Temple University Libraries, Urban Archives, Philadelphia, PA.

ened by the rising storm clouds of Soviet tanks, suggesting violent intervention to restore the old order of communism. "Old Line Stalinism" has been resurrected. Although the picnickers see the foreboding clouds, they appear oblivious to the threat facing them from the east.

A week later the *Christian Science Monitor* cartoon in Figure 13 portrays Soviet leader Leonid Brezhnev giving a stern warning to his Czechoslovak neighbors that their celebrated liberalizing policies are getting out of hand and need to be "toned down." If not, they will awaken other residents of the Soviet Bloc apartment complex, thus inviting increased trouble for him and Moscow in their attempt to keep them under control.

Figure 14 depicts a dejected, elderly Nikita Khrushchev, in retirement following his fall from Soviet power in 1964, watching on television the latest reforming events from Czechoslovakia. His wife smiles and knowingly states that "PAPA KNEW BEST!" Unlike his vacillating successor Brezhnev, he would have invaded Czechoslovakia early in the reform movement to end it as he had done in Hungary in 1956, as evidenced by the framed painting on the wall highlighting one of the major achievements of his rule.

The cartoonists resurrected the popular adage, "History repeats itself." Thirty years after an aggressive Nazi Germany occupied the Sudetenland region of Czechoslovakia, Figure 15 shows the Czechoslovak people once again unsuccessfully attempting to resist another invasion. They are no match for the powerful tanks of the Soviet Union which easily crushes them despite their unarmed attempts to resist. This cartoon follows the basic theme of earlier ones on events in 1948, seen in Figures 7 and 10, namely, that despite the efforts of the weak to resist, they are easily crushed by stronger, more powerful countries. Only the ideology of the oppressors has changed

In Figure 16, the ghosts of two previous repressors of Czechoslovakia, Adolf Hitler, who seized the Sudetenland in 1938 and annexed Czechoslovakia in 1939, and Joseph Stalin, who engineered the communist coup in 1948, gleefully hail the 1968 Soviet invasion in the person of the soldier Brezhnev. Brezhnev, with a smoking AK-47, has just shot down the unarmed body of peaceful democratic reforms of Czechoslovakia to restore oppression and dictatorship.

In Figure 17, the Warsaw Pact invaded Czechoslovakia to halt the reforms in Czechoslovakia, and to return the country to the "normalcy" of repression by the Soviet Union and complete control of the

Figure 12
Storm clouds?
Christian Science Monitor, 13 July 1968
Guernsey Le Pelley/© 1968 *The Christian Science Monitor*

Figure 13
'Pipe down ... I've got people sleeping ...'
Christian Science Monitor, 20 July 1968
Guernsey Le Pelley/© 1968 *The Christian Science Monitor*
(www.csmonitor.com). All rights reserved.

"PAPA KNEW BEST!"

Figure 14
"PAPA KNEW BEST!"
Philadelphia Inquirer, 1 August 1968.
www.pebsite.com

Invasion Of Czechoslovakia II

Figure 15
Invasion Of Czechoslovakia II
Chicago Sun Times, 22 August 1968
Copyright permission pending.

"On To The Past!"

Figure 16
"On To The Past!"
Washington Post, 22 August 1968
Copyright *Herblock: A Cartoonist's Life* (Time Books, 1998).

Figure 17
Back to Normalcy?
Taken from the *Philadelphia Inquirer*, 30 August 1968
Copyright permission pending.

Communist party. As a result, Czechoslovakia, after a brief experience with democracy, liberalism, and freedom, again faced the imprisonment of a communist system.

1989: A New Era

In 1989, Czechoslovakia became part of a larger process: the collapse of communism throughout East Central Europe. It was not the focal point of a crisis, but rather a part of a series of events that ended the Cold War. The rapid pace of the fall of communism in East Central European countries in domino-like fashion swamped the print and news media as shown in Figure 18.

Czechoslovakia was not and could not be singled out in political cartoons, but was represented within the context of the events occurring in East Central Europe. The "wicked witch" of communist oppression had finally melted in Figure 19. An unnamed Czechoslovakia joins with other anonymous East Bloc countries to celebrate the fall of communism.

In the autumn of 1989, events in East Central Europe moved quickly culminating for the West with the fall of the Berlin Wall, long a symbol of communist repression and the Cold War. Political cartoons focused on this symbol or tended to note the general rather than specific events as evidenced by Figure 20 and the previous two illustrations. Finally, Czechoslovakia has been freed from Soviet control. The focus now concentrated on immediate freedom and not past crises and difficulties. By early December 1989, only communist Romania remained in East Central Europe lamenting these changes, which would soon cause the collapse of that country's regime later that month. As shown by this last political drawing, after forty years of Soviet domination, the peoples and countries of East Central Europe (Poland, Hungary, Bulgaria, East Germany, and Czechoslovakia) had regained their sovereignty, with the exception of Romania. Romania, represented by an unkempt property and its slovenly owner clinging to the old communist ways, looks disgusted with the changes. Now, as masters of their own domains, the newly independent and democratic nations finally were able to put their houses in order after years of disrepair of communism.

Figure 18
"WE INTERRUPT THIS BULLETIN FROM BULGARIA – WHICH
INTERRUPTED THE BULLETIN FROM EAST BERLIN – WHICH
INTERRUPTED THE BULLETINS FROM MOSCOW AND POLAND
AND HUNGARY, TO BRING YOU THIS FROM CZECHOSLOVAKIA–"
Philadelphia Inquirer, 26 November 1989
Copyright *Herblock: A Cartoonist's Life* (Time Books, 1998).

Figure 19
DING DONG THE WITCH IS DEAD
Philadelphia Inquirer, 29 November 1989
AUTH © 1989 The Philadelphia Inquirer. Reprinted with permission of
UNIVERSAL PRESS SYNDICATE. All rights reserved.

Figure 20
.. SIGH .. THERE GOES TH' NEIGHBORHOOD
Philadelphia Inquirer, 3 December 1989
SARGENT © 1989 The Austin-American Statesman. Reprinted with
permission of UNIVERSAL PRESS SYNDICATE. All rights reserved.

CHAPTER 7

FINAL THOUGHTS

C ZECHOSLOVAKIA rose out of the ashes of the Habsburg monarchy at the end of the First World War in East Central Europe. Established on the principles of Wilsonian democracy by Thomas G. Masaryk and Edvard Beneš in October 1918, the small country became a hopeful beacon of democracy in the 1920s and 1930s, while states on its borders succumbed to dictatorships. Surrounded by hostile neighbors by the mid-1930s, Czechoslovakia formed defensive alliances with France (by implication also with Great Britain) and the Soviet Union. Buoyed by this protection, the Czechoslovaks believed they had nothing to fear especially with the rise of Adolf Hitler in Germany.

They were quickly mistaken. Twenty years after its 1918 founding in 1938, ten years later in 1948, again twenty years after that in 1968, and, finally, twenty-one years later in 1989, Czechoslovakia faced crises resulting from policies pursued by the Great Powers; its fate did not rest in its hands. Due to its size and location at the crossroads of Europe, Czechoslovakia became a mere pawn in great power politics and simply a bystander in directing its own fate.

The Great Depression of the 1930s and the increasing belligerent stance of Nazi Germany in violation of the Versailles Treaty of 1919 forced the European democracies of Britain and France to reassess their security commitments. Many statesmen now considered the treaty to be a mistake, and rather than spend precious money to uphold it, they preferred to let Hitler proceed while they used their shrinking resources elsewhere.

By 1938, Germany had rearmed, remilitarized the Rhineland, and annexed Austria while Britain and France stood by idly. After all, to many British and French leaders these moves just seemed natural for a country to regain its sovereignty. With Hitler's success in Austria, he started making demands on the Sudetenland, Czechoslovak territory where approximately three million Germans lived. The Czechoslovak government declared it would resist any attempts to detach any of its regions feeling secure with one of the better equipped and modernized militaries in Europe and backed by the alliances with France and the USSR.

Neither France, nor its partner Great Britain, wanted to fight for a country that had for them virtually no strategic interests, while the Soviet Union, claiming it would honor its alliance, in actuality had no inkling to do so. The British and French decided to negotiate rather than risk war leading to the Munich Agreement in September 1938, which British Prime Minister Neville Chamberlain called, "Peace in our time," which granted the Sudetenland to Germany. Czechoslovakia, not invited to the talks about its own territory, gave in after it realized its allies would not support it.

Americans read about and listened on the radio to these European events with great interest. In traditional American fashion, they sympathized with the "underdog" Czechoslovaks and their budding democracy, but feeling secure in their isolationist schizophrenia backed by the wide Atlantic Ocean, they did not want to intervene or challenge the policy of appeasement. Fearing another world war, Americans believed that their country should prepare, but were nonetheless shocked when it erupted.

Ten years later, after the British and French policy of appeasement failed to prevent the Second World War, Czechoslovakia faced another crisis. This time, in 1948, one of Czechoslovakia's allies from the war, the Soviet Union became the aggressor. After the hostilities, Czechoslovakia had a democratically elected government with a communist plurality. Despite its attempt to become a "bridge between the East and West," the Soviets feared that it leaned too far toward the West especially after the Czechoslovaks expressed interest in the American Marshall Plan in 1947. The Soviet Union finally moved to incorporate Czechoslovakia into its sphere in February 1948.

Despite the warning signs in the previous months, the February coup took most Americans by surprise, and many scholars consider the communist takeover of Czechoslovakia as a major cause of the Cold War which contributed to the formation of NATO. The American print media, as in 1938, supported the Czechoslovaks against the onslaught of its larger neighbor. Americans positively portrayed the people and the country which they felt embodied the values of the United States before the evil communists came to power: democracy, fair play, and political pragmatism. Czechoslovakia, in 1948, seemed a country with much in common with the United States, and one might have expected American intervention to uphold these values. Once again sympathy for the "little guy" became apparent, and certainly no country in East Central Europe identified as much with the traditions and values supported by Americans. However, America watched and criticized the coup, but, for a second time, did nothing.

After twenty years of communist rule, Czechoslovakia once more made it to the forefront of the American print media. This time, the Czechoslovak communists attempted to reform their system after a period of stagnation. Although American media attention remained relatively absent about the reform programs, it focused with the possibility of a Soviet invasion to end the changes. Americans applauded the transformations in Czechoslovakia and speculated about the possibilities of intervention. After the Warsaw Pact, under Soviet leadership, invaded the country, American sympathy arose once again for the tiny country abused by its brutal neighbors, especially the Soviet bear. Busy with a divisive presidential campaign and the Vietnam War, Americans quickly condemned invaders and, for a third time, forgot Czechoslovakia.

Twenty-one years later, in 1989, which the Czechoslovaks called "68 turned upside down," the country once more witnessed government-altering events. Czechoslovakia yet again faced the threat of possible intervention from its Soviet neighbor. This time, however, Czechoslovakia was not alone. Communism had begun to unravel in other Soviet satellite countries of East Central Europe months before it arrived in Czechoslovakia. As such, the event in the country became just one part of a larger, general trend with minor notice paid to it as compared to 1938, 1948, and 1968. None of these countries would have been able to proceed without the acquiescence of Soviet leader Mikhail Gorbachev. For Czechoslovakia, unusual since 1938, its fate now lay in its own hands. In the case of the collapse of communism in Czechoslovakia, it became submerged in the American print media by the fall of the Berlin Wall in November 1989. Americans saw the fall of communism in the Eastern bloc as part of their doing, but in actuality, they did little to foster such change in places like Czechoslovakia.

Events in 1938, 1948, 1968, and 1989 brought Czechoslovakia to the forefront of American news. Whether the country was democratic as in 1938 and 1948, or communist as in 1968 and 1989, Czechoslovakia stood for positive values against evil forces. Stronger dictatorial powers of Nazi Germany and the Soviet Union wanted to crush or could destroy the spirit of liberty and freedom, if they so desired. The American print media portrayed how Czechoslovakia attempted to remain and/or return to its own sovereignty with sympathy, but, except for 1989 expressed disappointment when it was brutally oppressed.

NOTES

CHAPTER 1

1. Successor states in Europe after the First World War, such as Czecho-slovakia, set up special departments to provide these correspondents positive information about these countries. The Czechoslovak government office is described by Halina Parafianowicz, "Vytváření obrazu Československé re-publiky v meziválečném období," (The Shaping of Images of the Czechoslo-vak Republic in the Interwar Period) in Luďa Klusáková, ed., *Obraz druhého v historické perspektivi* (The Image of the Second in Historical Perspective) (Prague: Univerzita Karlova, 1997), 67–85.

2. Bernard Cohen, *The Press & Foreign Policy* (Princeton: Princeton Uni-versity Press, 1963), 17. The most recent detailed analysis of foreign corre-spondents showed an ever more experienced and knowledgeable corps is Stephen Hess, *International News & Foreign Correspondents* (Washington, D.C.: The Brookings Institution, 1996). These findings were confirmed in a more narrowly-focused study by H. Denis Wu, "US Foreign Correspon-dents: Changes & Continuity at the Turn of the Century," *Gazette* 66:6 (December 2004): 517–32.

3. Slavomír Michálek, *Prípad Oatis: Československý komunistický režim verzus dopisovateľ Associated Press* (The Oatis Case: The Czechoslovak Communist Regime Versus the Associated Press Correspondent) (Bratislava: Ústav pamäti národa, 2005).

4. John Sheehan of CBS News reviewed for me the stories that had been aired on that same trip to Warsaw in 1985. Blood in the streets was a virtual necessity, he declared. In 1989, Jonathan Sanders, a consultant for CBS News, shared with me in Moscow his frustration over his New York editors' demands for pictures of lines for bread. "They don't understand," he said, "that while other goods might be in short supply, bread was not."

5. John Zaller and Dennis Chiu, "Government's Little Helper: U.S. Press

Coverage of Foreign Policy Crises, 1945–1991," *Political Communication* 13:4 (October-December 1996): 385–405.

6. David H. Weaver and G. Cleveland Wilhoit, as part of a larger international study, made a study of international news in the AP and UPI two decades ago, paying special attention to what trickled down to smaller newspapers: "Foreign News Coverage in two U.S. Wire Services," *Journal of Communication* 31:2 (Spring 1981): 55–63; and "Foreign News Coverage in Two U.S. Wire Services: An Update," *Journal of Communication* 33:2 (Spring 1983): 132–48.

7. Oscar S. Stauffer as quoted in "Home & Abroad Fall into One Pattern," *IPI Report* 1:8 (December 1952): 4.

8. For studies of the news agencies see Oliver Boyd-Barrett, *The International News Agencies* (London: Constable, 1980); and Jonathan Fenby, *The International News Services* (New York: Schocken, 1986).

9. Kyungmo Kim and George A. Barnett, "The Determinants of International News Flow: A Network Analysis," *Communication Research* 23:3 (June 1966): 324.

10. The pioneering work in this area of research was presented by Maxwell E. McCombs and Donald L. Shaw, "The Agenda-Setting Function of Mass Media," *Public Opinion Quarterly* 36:2 (Summer 1972): 176–87.

11. Wayne Wanta, Guy Golan, and Cheolhan Lee, "Agenda Setting & International News: Media Influence on Public Perceptions of Foreign Nations," *Journalism & Mass Communication Quarterly* 81:2 (Summer 2004): 364–77.

12. This assertion is supported by a recent experiment by Paul R. Brewer, Joseph Graf, and Lars Willnat, "Priming or Framing? Media Influence on Attitude Toward Foreign Countries," *Gazette* 65:6 (December 2003): 493–508. For background on media framing, see Todd Gitlin, *The Whole World Is Watching: Mass Media in the Making & Unmaking of the New Left* (Berkeley: University of California Press, 1980); Herbert J. Gans, *Deciding What's News: A Study of CBS Evening News, NBC Nightly News, Newsweek & Time* (New York: Pantheon, 1979); and Gaye Tuchman, *Making News: A Study in the Construction of Reality* (New York: The Free Press, 1978).

13. Michael B. MacKuen and Steven L. Coombs, *More Than News: Media Power in Public Affairs* (Beverly Hills, CA: Sage, 1981).

14. *The Flow of the News: A Study* (Zurich: International Press Institute, 1953).

15. Wilbur Schramm, *Mass Media and National Development* (Stanford, CA: Stanford University Press, 1964). Also see his *One Day in the World's*

Press (Stanford, CA: Stanford University Press, 1960).

16. Johan Galtung and Mari H. Ruge, "The Structure of Foreign News: The Presentation of the Congo, Cuba & Cyprus Crises in Four Norwegian Newspapers," *Journal of Peace Research* 2:1 (1965): 64-91.

17. Tsan-Kuo Chang, "All Countries Not Created Equal To Be News: World System and International Communication," *Communication Research* 25:5 (October 1998): 528-63.

18. J. D. Dupree, "International Communication: View From 'Window on the World'," *Gazette* 17:4 (1971): 224-35.

19. Einar Ostgaard, "Factors Influencing the Flow of News," *Journal of Peace Research* 2:1 (1965): 39-63.

20. Albert Hester, "Theoretical Considerations in Predicting Volume & Direction of International Information Flow," *Gazette* 19:4 (1973): 238-47.

21. UNESCO, *Many Voices, One World* (Paris: UNESCO, 1980).

22. Robert L. Stevenson and Donald L. Shaw, eds., *Foreign News & the New World Information Order* (Ames, IA: Iowa State University Press, 1984), and Annabelle Sreberny-Mohammadi, Kaarle Nordenstreng, Robert Stevenson, and Frank Ugboajah, "Foreign News in the Media: International News Reporting in 29 Countries," (UNESCO) *Reports & Papers in Mass Communication* No. 93 (1985).

23. K. Kyoon Hur, "A Critical Analysis of International News Flow Research," *Critical Studies in Mass Communication* 1:4 (December 1984): 365-78.

24. Tsan-Kuo Chang, Pamela Shoemaker, and Nancy Brendlinger, "Determinants of International News Coverage in the U.S. Media," *Communication Research* 14:4 (August 1987): 396-414. A more detailed examination of the impact of values is found in Christopher E. Beaudoin and Esther Thorson, "Value Representations in Foreign News," *Gazette* 63:6 (December 2001): 481-503.

25. Leonard L. Chu, "An Organizational Perspective on International News Flow: Some Generalizations, Hypotheses, & Questions for Research," *Gazette* 35:1 (1985): 3-18.

26. Pamela J. Shoemaker, *Gatekeeping* (Newbury Park, CA: Sage, 1991); Tsan-Kuo Chang and Jae-won Lee, "Factors Affecting Gatekeepers' Selection of Foreign News: A National Survey of Newspaper Editors," *Journalism Quarterly* 69:3 (Fall 1992): 554-61.

Notes to Chapter 1

27. Willard G. Bleyer, "The Press & Public Opinion in International Relations," *Journalism Bulletin* 3:2 (June 1926): 7.

28. Ibid., 13.

29. Owen V. Johnson, "Where is their Homeland? News about the Czechs & Their Lands in the U.S. Media, 1848–1914," in *Grossbritannien, die USA und die böhmischen Länder 1848–1938/Great Britain, the United States, and the Bohemian Lands 1848–1938*, eds. Eva Schmidt-Hartmann and Stanley B. Winters (Munich: R. Oldenbourg Verlag, 1991), 59–74.

30. Johnson, 74.

31. The most recent examination of this topic can be found in Tony Smith, *Foreign Attachments: The Power of Ethnic Groups in the Making of American Foreign Policy* (Cambridge, MA: Harvard University Press, 2000).

32. Paul F. Douglass and Karl Bömer, "The Press as a Factor in International Relations," *Annals of the American Academy of Political and Social Science* 162 (July 1932): 241–72.

33. Leland Stowe, "The Press & International Friction," *Journalism Quarterly* 13:1 (March 1936): 1–6.

34. Reginald Coggeshall, "Diplomatic Implications in International News," *Journalism Quarterly* 11:2 (June 1934): 141–59.

35. Owen V. Johnson, "Ernie's Letters," a book manuscript in progress, examines more than 1,000 of Pyle's extant letters in several archival collections and in private hands.

36. George F. Kennan, *Memoirs, 1925–1950* (Boston: Little Brown, 1967), 403.

37. Joseph C. Harsch, *Does Our Foreign Policy Make Sense?* (New York: Foreign Policy Association, 1948), 17, 57.

38. Gabriel Almond, *The American People & Foreign Policy* (New York: Frederick A. Praeger, 1963), 91–98.

39. In July 1990, a group of leading American editors came to Prague to meet with the new editors of various East Central European publications. I had the privilege of observing these discussions, which included such notables as Arthur Sulzberger, Jr. of the *New York Times*, Ben Bradlee of the *Washington Post*, Sander Vanocur of *ABC News*, and veteran writer David Halberstam. Czechoslovak President Václav Havel addressed one of the sessions. On another occasion, American Ambassador Shirley Temple Black invited all of us to her residence for informal discussions with Czechoslovak Foreign Min-

ister and former dissident Jiří Dienstbier. The Americans seemed blissfully unaware of the complexities of life in Czechoslovakia under communism and pounced on Havel's press secretary for suggesting that the Czechoslovak government opposed the publication of unverified lists of alleged collaborators with the secret police. Owen V. Johnson, "Czech Presidential Press Secretary Apologizes," *Editor and Publisher* 123:38 (22 September 1990): 26.

40. Mark W. Summers, "American Cartoonists & a World of Revolutions, 1789–1936," in *Media & Revolution: Comparative Perspectives*, ed. Jeremy D. Popkin (Lexington: University Press of Kentucky, 1995): 150–51,

41. Walter Lippmann, *Public Opinion* (New York: Harcourt, Brace and Co., 1922; reprint The Free Press, 1965), 229.

CHAPTER 2

1. Raymond Fielding, *The March of Time, 1935–1951* (New York: Oxford University Press, 1978), 139, 230.

2. U.S., Department of Commerce, Bureau of the Census, *Historical Statistics of the United States: Colonial Times to 1970. Part 1* (Washington D.C., Government Printing Office, 1975), 383.

3. "American Institute of Public Opinion-Survey, 1938–1939," *Public Opinion Quarterly* 3 (October 1939): 603.

4. Alice M. Dougan, Bertha Joel, and Jeannette Moore-Smith, eds., *Readers' Guide to Periodical Literature: An Author and Subject Index July 1937– June 1939* (New York: The H. W. Wilson Company, 1939), 460–63, 1231. It should to be noted that there is some article overlap between the respective topics.

5. *N. W. Ayer and Son's American Newspaper Annual and Directory* (Philadelphia: N. W. Ayer and Son, 1938). The reported figures and the pages this information can be found for newspapers are *Baltimore Sun*: 142,904 (375); *Chicago Tribune*: 822,486 (215); *Honolulu Advertiser*: 15,001 (179); *Los Angeles Times*: 215,768 (86); *New Orleans Times-Picayune*: 121,233 (362); *New York Times*: 515,343 (640); *Pittsburgh Courier*: 145,022 (797); *Salisbury Times*: 3,509 (379); and *Wall Street Journal*: 33,104 (642). As for the magazines: *Independent Woman*: 60,291; *Life*: 1,000,895 (208); *National Republic*: 32,000 (643); *New Republic*: 26,948 (629); *Newsweek*: 277,899 (630); *New Yorker*: 134,661 (630); and *Time*: 670,341 (215).

6. *New York Times*, 2 September 1938; *Honolulu Advertiser*, 3 September 1938.

7. *Honolulu Advertiser*, 17 February 1980.

8. *Honolulu Advertiser*, 3 September 1938.

9. *Los Angeles Times*, 7 September 1938.

10. *New Orleans Times-Picayune*, 1 September 1938.

11. *Los Angeles Times*, 14 September 1938.

12. *Baltimore Sun*, 5 September 1938.

13. *Los Angeles Times*, 2 September 1938.

14. *Current Biography: Who's News and Why 1943* (New York: H. W. Wilson, 1944), 160–62.

15. Vera Micheles Dean, "Europe Wants Peace," *Independent Woman*, September 1938, 275, 303 cont.

16. Radomír Luža, *The Transfer of the Sudeten Germans: A Study of Czech-German Relations, 1933–1962* (New York: New York University Press, 1964), 138–40.

17. Ibid.

18. *New York Times*, 7 September 1938.

19. *Baltimore Sun*, 9 September 1938.

20. "LIFE on the Newsfronts of the World," *Life*, 19 September 1938, 14.

21. *Wall Street Journal*, 9 September 1938.

22. Howard Brubaker, "Of All Things," *New Yorker*, 17 September 1938, 43.

23. *Baltimore Sun*, 10 September 1938.

24. *New Orleans Times-Picayune*, 10 September 1938.

25. *Los Angeles Times*, 11 September 1938.

26. *New York Times*, 8 September 1938.

27. "LIFE on the Newsfronts of the World," *Life*, 5 September 1938, 14-15.

28. *New York Times*, 9 September 1938.

29. Ibid., 10 September 1938.

30. Ibid.

31. *New Orleans Times-Picayune*, 10 September 1938.

32. "Britain Moves on Two Fronts to Protect Czechoslovakia," *Newsweek*, 12 September 1938, 16.

33. *New York Times*, 11 September 1938.

34. "Foreign News," *Time*, 12 September 1938, 29.

35. T.R.B., "Washington Notes," *New Republic*, 14 September 1938, 158.

36. *Chicago Tribune*, 6 September 1938.

37. Barbara Rearden Farnham, *Roosevelt and the Munich Crisis: A Study of Political Decision-Making* (Princeton: Princeton University Press, 1997), 98 n. 25.

38. "Administration Warns World Against Presuming U.S. Course," *Newsweek*, 19 September 1938, 9–10.

39. *New York Times*, 11 September 1938.

40. Ibid., 13 September 1938.

41. "Foreign News," *Time*, 19 September 1938, 19.

42. *Baltimore Sun*, 12 September 1938.

43. "Strategy Underlies Defiance in Hitler's Address to the World," *Newsweek*, 19 September 1938, 14.

44. *Baltimore Sun*, 13 September 1938.

45. Ibid., 12 September 1938.

46. Howard Brubaker, "Of All Things," *New Yorker*, 17 September 1938, 43.

47. "Foreign News," *Time*, 19 September 1938, 20.

48. *New Orleans Times-Picayune*, 12 September 1938.

49. "LIFE on the Newsfronts of the World," *Life*, 12, 19 September 1938, 16, 14.

50. "The Fate of Europe Turns on the Bavarian Terrace of Reichsfuhrer Hitler," *Life*, 26 September 1938, 13.

51. *Chicago Tribune*, 14 September 1938; *Los Angeles Times*, 13 September 1938; *New Orleans Times-Picayune*, 14 September 1938.

52. *Honolulu Advertiser*, 13 September 1938; *New York Times*, 13 September 1938; *Baltimore Sun*, 13 September 1938.

53. *Los Angeles Times*, 13 September 1938.

54. *New York Times*, 14 September 1938.

55. "The Fate of Europe Turns on the Bavarian Terrace of Reichsfuhrer Hitler," *Life*, 26 September 1938, 18–19.

56. *Salisbury Times*, 12 September 1938.

57. "Strategy Underlies Defiance in Hitler's Address to the World," *Newsweek*, 19 September 1938, 16.

58. Howard Brubaker, "Of All Things," *New Yorker*, 17 September 1938, 43.

59. *Salisbury Times*, 12 September 1938.

60. *New Orleans Times-Picayune*, 15 September 1938.

61. *Los Angeles Times*, 14 September 1938.

62. *Wall Street Journal*, 15 September 1938.

63. Henry Steele Commanger and Milton Cantor, eds., *Documents of American History: Volume II Since 1898*, tenth edition (Englewood Cliffs, NJ: Prentice Hall, 1988), 378–82.

64. *Wall Street Journal*, 19 September 1938.

65. *Chicago Tribune*, 16 September 1938.

66. *New York Times*, 15 September 1938; *Baltimore Sun*, 15 September 1938; *Honolulu Advertiser*, 15 September 1938; *Life*, 26 September 1938, 16.

67. "Foreign News," *Time*, 26 September 1938, 15.

68. *New York Times*, 16 September 1938; *Baltimore Sun*, 19 September 1938; *New Orleans Times-Picayune*, 16 September 1938; *Honolulu Advertiser*, 18 September 1938.

69. *New York Times*, 16 September 1938; *Baltimore Sun*, 19 September 1938; *Honolulu Advertiser*, 18 September 1938.

70. *New York Times*, 16 September 1938; *Baltimore Sun*, 17 September 1938.

71. *New Orleans Times-Picayune*, 16 September 1938; 17 September 1938.

72. Genêt, "Letter from Budapest," *New Yorker*, 24 September 1938, 45–47.

73. "The Fate of Europe Turns on the Bavarian Terrace of Reichsfuhrer Hitler," *Life*, 26 September 1938, 20.

74. *New York Times*, 18 September 1938.

75. Igor Lukes, *Czechoslovakia between Stalin and Hitler: The Diplomacy of Edvard Beneš in the 1930s* (New York: Oxford University Press, 1996), 213–22.

76. *Baltimore Sun*, 19 September 1938.

77. Ibid., 20 September 1938.

78. Ibid.

79. *New Orleans Times-Picayune*, 20 September 1938; 22 September 1938.

80. *Los Angeles Times*, 18 September 1938; 21 September 1938.

81. "The Great Surrender," *New Republic*, 28 September 1938, 200–201.

82. *Honolulu Advertiser*, 20 September 1938.

83. *Salisbury Times*, 20 September 1938; 21 September 1938.

84. *New York Times*, 20 September 1938.

85. *Los Angeles Times*, 20 September 1938.

86. *Wall Street Journal*, 20 September 1938.

87. *New York Times*, 21 September 1938.

88. *Baltimore Sun*, 21 September 1938.

89. *New Orleans Times-Picayune*, 25 September 1938.

90. *Chicago Tribune*, 22 September 1938.

91. *New York Times*, 22 September 1938.

92. "Democracies' Uncertainty Gives Hitler His Greatest Triumph," *Newsweek*, 26 September 1938, 17.

93. *Los Angeles Times*, 22 September 1938; 23 September 1938.

94. "LIFE on the Newsfronts of the World," *Life*, 3 October 1938, 24.

95. *Los Angeles Times*, 23 September 1938.

96. Howard Brubaker, "Of All Things," *New Yorker*, 1 October 1938, 32.

97. *Los Angeles Times*, 24 September 1938; 25 September 1938.

98. *New York Times*, 7 September 1942.

99. Ludwig Lore, "On the European Front," *Independent Woman*, October 1938, 306, 331 cont.

100. *New Orleans Times-Picayune*, 27 October 1938; 28 September 1938.

101. *Chicago Tribune*, 28 September 1938.

102. *Honolulu Advertiser*, 27 September 1938.

103. *Baltimore Sun*, 27 September 1938.

104. *New York Times*, 27 September 1938; *Baltimore Sun*, 26 September 1938.

105. *Los Angeles Times*, 27 September 1938.

106. "The Periscope," *Newsweek*, 26 September 1938, 7; 3 October 1938, 9; 10 October 1938, 5.

107. "National Affairs," "Foreign News," *Time*, 26 September 1938, 10, 17.

108. Howard Brubaker, "Of All Things," *New Yorker*, 1 October 1938, 32.

109. *Baltimore Sun*, 27 September 1938.

110. *New York Times*, 28 September 1938.

111. Howard Brubaker, "Of All Things," *New Yorker*, 8 October 1938, 29.

112. "The Week," *New Republic*, 12 October 1938, 253.

113. "The Periscope," *Newsweek*, 3 October 1938, 10.

114. *Chicago Tribune*, 27 September 1938.

115. *Wall Street Journal*, 27 September 1938.

116. *New York Times*, 25 September 1938.

117. *Honolulu Advertiser*, 29 September 1938; *Baltimore Sun*, 29 September 1938; *Los Angeles Times*, 29 September 1938; *New York Times*, 29 September 1938.

118. *Chicago Tribune*, 29 September 1938.

119. *Wall Street Journal*, 29 September 1938.

120. "The Talk of the Town," *New Yorker*, 1 October 1938, 7.

121. Farnham, *Roosevelt and the Munich Crisis*, 138.

122. 'The Periscope," *Newsweek*, 10 October 1938, 5.

123. "Britain's Peace With Honor," *Newsweek*, 17.

124. *New York Times*, 30 September 1938.

125. *Chicago Tribune*, 30 September 1938; 1 October 1938.

126. *Honolulu Advertiser*, 2 October 1938.

127. *New Orleans Times-Picayune*, 30 September 1938.

128. *Los Angeles Times*, 30 September 1938.

129. *Life*, 3 October 1938, 20; 10 October 1938, 11–13, 19, 60.

130. *Wall Street Journal*, 1 October 1938.

131. Genêt, "Letter from Paris," *New Yorker*, 8 October 1938, 30–31.

132. Ibid., 29.

133. *Baltimore Sun*, 30 September 1938.

134. "The Week," *New Republic*, 12 October 1938, 253.

135. *Los Angeles Times*, 2 October 1938.

136. "War Scare," *National Republic*, October 1938, 12.

137. *New York Times*, 31 January 1958.

138. Clyde Eagleton, "Aftermanth of the 'Surrender' at Munich," *Independent Woman*, November 1938, 339, 364 cont.

139. "Times Change," *National Republic*, November 1938, 11–12.

140. *Pittsburgh Courier,* 8 October 1938.

141. Ibid., 15 October 1938.

142. George Gallup and Claude Robinson, "American Institute of Public Opinion-Surveys, 1935–1938," *Public Opinion Quarterly* 2 (July 1938): 373.

143. George Gallup, "Testing Public Opinion," *Public Opinion Quarterly. Special Supplement: Public Opinion in a Democracy* 2 (January 1938): 9.

144. George Gallup, *The Gallup Poll: Public Opinion 1935–1971*, edited by William P. Hansen and Fred L. Israel (New York: Random House, 1972), 1: 120–23, 131–32.

145. "American Institutie of Public Opinion-Survey, 1938–1939," *Public Opinion Quarterly* 3 (October 1939): 598.

146. Gallup, *The GallupPoll*, 1: 120–23, 131–32.

147. *Chicago Tribune*, September 2, 1939.

CHAPTER 3

1. I would like to thank the Summer Research Laboratory for Russian and East European Studies at the University of Illinois for its support of this topic.

2. *The World Almanac and Book of Facts for 1949* (New York: New York World-Telegram, 1949). The rankings of the circulation of the 25 leading magazines of the United States placed *Time* at number 23. *Reader's Digest* ranked first, *Life* second, and *Saturday Evening Post* fourth.

3. For discussions on the complexity of this issue see: James Aronson, *The Press and the Cold War* (Indianapolis: Bobbs-Merrill Co., 1970) and Louis Liebovich, *The Press and the Origins of the Cold War, 1944-1947* (New York: Praeger, 1988).

4. Liebovich, 140. Nancy E. Bernhard writes, "Diplomatic reporting had long been dominated by informal insider journalism, where reporters and senior officers cultivated one another in background briefings and at private clubs." Nancy E. Bernhard, "Clearer than Truth: Public Affairs Television and the State Department's Domestic Information Campaigns," *Diplomatic History* 21 (Fall 1997): 545–46.

5. George E. Simmons, "The 'CW' in Large City Dailies of the U.S.," *Journalism Quarterly* 25 (December 1948): 354-359, 400.

6. Raymond Daniel, "Crossroads Between Two Worlds," *New York Times Magazine*, 26 October 1947, 60.

7. *New York Times*, 18 November 1947.

8. Ibid., 9 February 1948.

9. Frank Costigliola, "The Nuclear Family: Tropes of Gender and Pathology in the Western Alliance," *Diplomatic History* 21 (Spring 1997):163–183. Also see "Culture, Gender, and Foreign Policy: A Symposium," *Diplomatic History* 18 (Winter 1994): 47–124.

10. The popular news media seldom made ethnic distinctions regarding the peoples of Czechoslovakia who included Czechs, Slovaks, Germans, Ruthenians, and Hungarians. The nation-state was referred to as Czechoslovakia and its people as Czechs. Almost all news pictures dealt with the Czech Lands of Bohemia and Moravia and the city of Prague, in particular.

11. *Austin Statesman*, 24 February 1948.

12. *Chicago Daily News*, 23 February 1948.

13. *New York Times*, 5 August 1947.

14. *St. Louis Post-Dispatch*, 11 March 1948.

15. *San Francisco Chronicle*, 14 March 1948; *New York Times*, 7 March 1948, 29 February 1948, 24 February 1948; *U.S. News & World Report*, 25 November 1947, 20; 30 December 1947, 11.

16. *Chicago Daily News*, 28 February 1948; *Christian Science Monitor*, 2 March 1948; *Austin American*, 28 February 1948; *Christian Science Monitor*, 27 February 1948; *New York Times*, 29 May 1948.

17. *Austin Statesman*, 24 February 1948.

18. *San Francisco Chronicle*, 13 March 1948.

19. *St. Louis Post-Dispatch*, 25 February 1948.

20. *New York Times*, 9 February 1948.

21. Ibid., 18 November 1947.

22. *San Francisco Chronicle*, 24 February 1948.

23. *St. Louis Post-Dispatch*, 22 February 1948.

24. Ibid.

25. G.E.R. Gedye, "Behind the Struggle for Czechoslovakia," *Nation*, 28 February 1948, 230.

26. Freda Kirchwey, "Prague—a Lesson for Liberals," *Nation*, 6 March 1948, 265.

27. "What Happened in Prague," *New Republic*, 8 March 1948, 12. Irving D.W. Talmadge, "Czechoslovakia: Moscow's Reluctant Ally," *Current History*, November 1970, 270.

28. Hans Kohn, "Democracy in the Soviet Orbit: Czechoslovakia's Struggle," *Current History*, February 1948, 68. He did note that "present day Czechoslovakia is not a democracy in the full sense of the word," because certain freedoms, such as freedom of the press, were lacking.

29. *New York Times*, 1 February 1947.

30. Ibid., 2 February 1947.

31. Victor Seroff, "Grace Under Pressure," *New Republic*, 16 July 1947, 15.

32. *Chicago Daily News*, 16 February 1948; 28 February 1948. Masaryk's mother was an American, while Beneš had visited the country several times and had family members living in the United States.

33. *New York Times,* 7 May 1947.

34. *Chicago Tribune,* 12 January 1948.

35. *St. Louis Globe-Democrat,* 26 February 1948. The Pittsburgh Pact of May 1918 was not a constitution, but rather an agreement for the Czechs and Slovaks to live in one state.

36. David Scott, "Czech Rubber Stamp," *New Republic,* 7 June 1948, 14.

37. Frederick H. Cramer, "Between East and West," *Forum,* July 1948, 9. The cartoon originally appeared in the *Evening Bulletin* (Philadelphia), 9 June 1948. See Figure 11 in the last chapter for a copy of this cartoon.

38. *Chicago Tribune,* 27 February 1948.

39. *Chicago Daily News,* 28 February 1948.

40. *San Francisco Chronicle,* 27 February 1948.

41. *St. Louis Post-Dispatch,* 25 February 1948.

42. Ibid., 11 March 1948.

43. *Atlanta Constitution,* 27 February 1948. "The Space For Freedom Grows Smaller," *Newsweek,* 8 March 1948, 28.

44. *Christian Science Monitor,* 27 February 1948.

45. *San Francisco Chronicle,* 7 March 1948.

46. *Chicago Daily News,* 4 March 1948.

47. Ibid., 15 March 1948.

48. Ibid., 12 March 1948.

49. *St. Louis Globe-Democrat,* 26 February 1948; 1 March 1948; 13 March 1948.

50. "The Death Of A Wilsonian Republic," *Newsweek,* 8 March 1948, 17.

51. "For Centuries Czechs Have Waged Discouraging Battle For Victory," *Life,* 8 March 1948, 28–29.

52. "What Happened In Prague," *New Republic,* 8 March 1948, 12.

53. Gedye, *Nation,* 28 February 1948, 230.

54. *New York Times,* 13 June 1948.

55. *Chicago Tribune,* 14 March 1948.

56. *San Francisco Chronicle,* 28 February 1948. See Figure 10 in the last chapter for a copy of this cartoon.

57. Ibid., 24 February 1948.

58. *New York Times,* 9 August 1947.

59. Albion Ross, "Iron Curtains For Czechoslovakia," *Reader's Digest,* May 1948, 36.

60. "The Death Of A Wilsonian Republic," *Newsweek,* 8 March 1948, 17. *Atlanta Constitution,* 27 February 1948.

61. Cramer, *Forum,* July 1948, 9. See Figure 11 in the last chapter for a copy of this cartoon.

62. *New York Times,* 11 May 1947.

63. *San Francisco Chronicle,* 26 February 1948.

64. Ibid., 1 March 1948.

65. Ibid., 26 February 1948.

66. *St. Louis Post-Dispatch,* 13 March 1948.

67. *St. Louis Globe-Democrat,* 25 February 1948.

68. "U.S. Foreign Policy Takes A Licking," *Life,* 8 March 1948, 27.

69. Gedye, *Nation,* 28 February 1948, 230. *St. Louis Post-Dispatch,* 9 March 1948. These reports of Beneš's ill health were disputed by Stanley Winters, "The Health of Edvard Beneš: An Unpublished Letter from 1948," *East Central Europe* 4 (1977): 60–66. Also see Edward Taborsky, "President Edvard Beneš and the Crises of 1938 and 1948," *East Central Europe* 5 (1978): 213. The evidence challenging accusations of Beneš's health hindering his decision-making powers are based on the papers of Jaromír Smutný, an aide to Beneš. A Soviet NKVD agent who had a fifteen minute meeting with Beneš during the crisis reported that Beneš was a "broken, ailing man...." Pavel and Anatoli Sudoplatov, *Special Tasks: The Memoirs of An Unwanted Witness—A Soviet Spymaster* (Boston: Little, Brown and Company, 1994): 234.

70. *St. Louis Post-Dispatch,* 4 March 1948.

71. *St. Louis Globe-Democrat,* 26 February 1948.

72. Demaree Bess, "Roosevelt's Secret Deal Doomed Czechoslovakia: At Yalta and Before," *Saturday Evening Post,* 17 April 1948, 26. This article described parallels between FDR's and Beneš's relationships with the Soviets.

73. *New York Times*, 29 February 1948.

74. *St. Louis Post-Dispatch*, 2 March 1948.

75. Ibid. In actuality, a treaty between Czechoslovakia and the Soviet Union was signed on December 12, 1943. It was a matter of public knowledge.

76. Sudoplatov, *Special Tasks*, 104, 223, 233. Sudoplatov in several instances uses the term "agent" loosely, sometimes meaning a person who could be influenced by Moscow. Beneš was trying to use the Soviets, and Sudoplatov may have assumed more control than actually existed in Beneš's mind. However, Sudoplatov does describe a secret visit in 1948 by himself, four hundred Special Purpose troops dressed in civilian attire, and Pyotr Zubov, an NKVD agent said to be Beneš's control officer to signal Beneš that he should cooperate with Gottwald. Sudoplatov assumed that the NKVD had enough knowledge of Beneš past cooperation with Soviet agents to blackmail him. After the signal had been communicated to Beneš, Beneš's resistance to the communist takeover disintegrated.

77. *San Francisco Chronicle*, 11 March 1948; 16 March 1948. Joseph B. Phillips, "Tales From Czechoslovakia," *Newsweek*, 29 March 1948, 38. *St. Louis Post-Dispatch*, 10 March 1948.

78. *San Francisco Chronicle*, 14 March 1948.

79. Ibid.

80. *Chicago Daily News*, 12 March 1948.

81. *St. Louis Post-Dispatch*, 10 March 1948.

82. Ibid., 5 March 1948.

83. Joseph B. Phillips, "Tales From Czechoslovakia," *Newsweek*, 29 March 1948, 38. Schweik, the lead character in *The Good Soldier Schweik*, written by Jaroslav Hašek in the 1920s, has become synonymous with the Czech tendency to confront political oppression with passive resistance and the ability to protest in a unique way against the authorities rather than outright rebellion.

84. *Chicago Daily News*, 12 March 1948; *San Francisco Chronicle*, 11 March 1948—see Figure 9 in the last chapter for a copy of this cartoon.

85. *St Louis Globe-Democrat*, 26 February 1948.

86. *Chicago Daily News*, 12 March 1948. The author of the article, Dorothy Thompson, quoted Masaryk saying, "I feel like a swine. I am a stinking coward." However, in the same column she said that Masaryk told her that he would not sell his soul and mind.

87. *San Francisco Chronicle*, 16 March 1948. Edgar A. Mowrer, the author of this article, felt that Wallace, like Masaryk, was "hopelessly obtuse on one subject, the Soviet Union." Strangely, Mowrer felt that Masaryk in death, "saved his honor." An editorial in the *St. Louis Globe-Democrat*, 11 March 1948, stated that Masaryk "has now made amends" for his past lack of political will.

88. Edward R. Murrow, "Jan Masaryk," *New Republic*, 22 March 1948, 8. This article was a printed copy of Murrow's March 10 news analysis on CBS radio.

89. *Chicago Tribune*, 26 February 1948.

90. *New York Times*, 5 August 1947.

91. *San Francisco Chronicle*, 26 February 1948; "The Space For Freedom Grows Smaller," *Newsweek*, 8 March 1948, 28. This article reported Beneš as responding to Gottwald's intimidation by saying, "You're talking to me like Hitler." A similar quote also appeared in the *San Francisco Chronicle*, 27 February 1948.

92. San Francisco Chronicle, 2 March 1948.

93. *St. Louis Post-Dispatch*, 25 February 1948.

94. Ibid.

95. "Coupe Takes Place Against Background Of Crowds And Fiery Speeches," *Life*, 8 March 1948, 30.

96. A later discussion of the complexities of Gottwald's maneuvering and policies is described by Radomír V. Luža, "February 1948 and the Czechoslovak Road to Socialism," *East Central Europe* 4 (1977): 44-55. Also see "Gottwald: Czechoslovak Premier," *World Report*, 29 July 1947.

97. *Atlanta Constitution*, 11 March 1948. The article's headline read: "Shake Fist At Reds, Avert Munich." The article quoted Ellis Arnall, a former governor of Georgia, saying that "the United States must put its foot down on another Munich and tell Russia firmly and emphatically that this nation is determined to fight...." In an article in the *San Francisco Chronicle*, 28 February 1948, with a headline "Bidault Asserts Czech Action Is Threat To Europe," the French foreign minister saw Europe going back to Hitler's time. On the same page, Secretary of Commerce Averill Harriman was the source of a headline "Russia Called Bigger Peril Than Hitler." The 7 March 1948 issue of the *San Francisco Chronicle* contained the headline reading "Strong Policy or Another Munich, Says Morse" and summarized the Oregon's senator's feelings. A column by Constantine Brown in the *St. Louis Globe-Democrat*, 27 February 1948, presents the case that Stalin was even doing a better job than Hitler at taking territory without consequences.

98. *New York Times*, 13 June 1948. *Chicago Tribune*, 4 March 1948.

99. David Lawrence, "Aggression That Could Mean War," *U.S. News & World Report*, 12 March 1948, 38.

100. E.N. Harmon and Milton MacKaye, "Fighting General Tells His Story," *Saturday Evening Post*, 9 October 1948, 28, 143 cont.; *Atlanta Constitution*, 26 February 1948; *Chicago Tribune*, 27 February 1948. The article's headline read: "Marshall Says It's Untrue U.S. Refused To Help Free Czechs." *Chicago Daily News*, 1 March 1948, contained the article headline: "Prague? That's City We Let Reds Free." *St. Louis Globe-Democrat*, 26 February 1948, published a headline reading: "Czech Fall May Reveal Many U.S. War Secrets."

101. *New York Times*, 29 February 1948. The article called the move the "most dramatic victory yet scored by the foreign policy of the Soviet Union." It also argued that Moscow does not want to build bridges to the West. An editorial in the *San Francisco Chronicle*, 27 February 1948, called the idea of a bridge between East and West a delusion. "The Death Of A Wilsonian Republic," *Newsweek*, 8 March 1948, 17, also argued that "the effort of the Czechs to act as a bridge between East and West and to reconcile freedom with Communism had come to an end ... not with a bang but a whimper."

102. *St. Louis Globe-Democrat*, 22 February 1948. This was a secondary headline. The lead headline read "Czech Crisis Traced To Russian Plot."

103. *San Francisco Chronicle*, 1 March 1948.

104. *Atlanta Constitution*, 7 March 1948; *San Francisco Chronicle*, 29 February 1948; *St. Louis Post-Dispatch*, 7 March 1948. The *San Francisco Chronicle* cited Ferenc Nagy, a former Hungarian premier, with similar concerns on 26 February 1948: the headline read "'Austria, Italy, France Next,' Nagy Predicts." "A Tense World Asks Who Is Next," *Newsweek*, 15 March 1948, 29; "Peace: War Fears Grip Capital and Nation," 22 March 1948, 23.

105. *Austin American*, 27 February 1948, led with the headline "Western Europe Jittery. US, Britain, France Hit Coup; More Seizures Expected." The secondary headline read "Who's Next?" The *Austin Statesman*, 28 February 1948, ran a headline "With Czechoslovakia in The Bag, Finland Maybe Next, Diplomatic Observers." The headline of the *Atlanta Constitution*, 27 February 1948, read "Czech Success—Next?" The 1 March 1948 issue of the *Atlanta Constitution* contained headlines over two articles with one reading "U.S. Warned To Stop Reds Or Face 'World Revolution'" and the other "Collision With U.S. Seen In More Red Expansions." The *Chicago Tribune*, 27 February 1948, argued in an editorial that Italy was next and on 28 February 1948 described Stalin's pressure on Finland.

106. *St. Louis Post-Dispatch*. 2 March 1948.

107. *Chicago Tribune*, 26 February 1948, 1 March 1948, 2 March 1948, 11 March 1948; *San Francisco Chronicle*, 18 February 1948, 1 March 1948; *St. Louis Globe-Democrat*, 2 March 1948; *St. Louis Post-Dispatch*, 6 March 1948; *New York Times*, 29 February 1948, 14 March 1948; *Salisbury Times*, 6 March 1948, see Figure 6 in the last chapter for this cartoon.

108. *Christian Science Monitor*, 28 February 1948.

109. *St. Louis Globe-Democrat*, 28 February 1948. The author, David Lawrence, in a later column in another newspaper speculated that "Russia has overplayed her hand." *Chicago Daily News*, 15 March 1948. A news article in the *San Francisco Chronicle*, 6 March 1948, also discussed the possibility that Moscow's failure to run Czechoslovakia will show the failure of communism.

110. *San Francisco Chronicle*, 3 March 1948.

111. "What Happened In Prague," *New Republic*, 8 March 1948, 12.

112. *San Francisco Chronicle*, 27 February 1948.

113. Ibid., 28 February 1948.

114. *St. Louis Globe-Democrat*, 2 March 1948.

115. "Whispers," *U.S. News & World Report*, 12 March 1948, 72.

116. *New York Times*, 2 March 1948; *Atlanta Constitution*, 29 February 1948. "The Death Of A Wilsonian Republic," *Newsweek*, 8 March 1948, 17.

117. *San Francisco Chronicle*, 29 February 1948. The paper quoted Taft arguing that "a military coup and that sort of thing is not stopped by financial aid," 15 March 1948.

118. George Weller, "Soviet Coup in Prague. Argument Against Marshall Plan," *San Francisco Chronicle*, 28 February 1948.

119. *New York Times*, 18 March 1948. Wallace charged that the United States ambassador to Czechoslovakia, Laurence A. Steinhardt, "had been prevented by one day from bringing about a 'rightist coup' in Prague." Steinhardt responded by saying Wallace received this false information from his "Communist associates." *San Francisco Chronicle*, 3 March 1948; 18 March 1948.

120. *Atlanta Constitution*, 28 February 1948.

121. *San Francisco Chronicle*, 1 March 1948.

122. Ibid., 16 March 1948.

123. *St. Louis Globe-Democrat*, 25 February 1948. An editorial in the *St. Louis Post-Dispatch*, 26 February 1948, argued that Beneš was mistaken to work with the Soviets.

124. *St. Louis Globe-Democrat*, 13 March 1948.

125. *St. Louis Post-Dispatch*, 26 February 1948.

126. Ibid., 11 March 1948.

127. "What Happened In Prague," *New Republic*, 8 March 1948, 12–13. "Footnote to Czechoslovakia," *New Republic*, 22 March 1948, 39. David Scott, "Czech Rubber Stamp," *New Republic*, 7 June 1948, 14. Freda Kirchwey, *Nation*, 6 March 1948, 265–66.

128. James F. Byrnes, *Speaking Frankly* (New York: Harper, 1947): 143. "Footnote," *New Republic*, 22 March 1948, 39.

129. Frank Kofsky, *Harry S. Truman and the War Scare of 1948: A Successful Campaign to Deceive the Nation* (New York: St. Martin's Press, 1995). Kofsky details the Truman administration's manipulation of these events to create a crisis so that Congress would pass the Marshall Plan and approve universal military training. Also see Walter Isaacson and Evan Thomas, *The Wise Men: Six Friends and the World They Made* (New York: Simon & Schuster, 1986), 439–40.

130. *San Francisco Chronicle*, 27 February 1948. *Atlanta Constitution*, 1 March 1948.

131. *St. Louis Globe-Democrat*, 1 March 1948; *St. Louis Post-Dispatch*, 4 March 1948, 15 March 1948.

132. *Chicago Tribune*, 11 March 1948; San Francisco, 11 March 1948.

133. *Chicago Daily News*, 23 February 23, 1948. The author, Wallace R. Duel, also said that "neither the United States nor any other power will even try to do anything effective to prevent the Soviets from establishing total control over Czechoslovakia...." The same column appeared in the *San Francisco Chronicle*, 24 February 1948. George F. Kennan, *Memoirs, 1925–1950* (Boston: Little, Brown and Company, 1967), 379. Kennan believed Moscow would eventually take over Czechoslovakia. Reports from the American ambassador in Prague also indicated the likelihood of a communist takeover months before the actual events occurred. Kofsky, *War Scare of 1948*, 93–95.

134. *San Francisco Chronicle*, 1 March 1948.

135. "Building Up The Soviet Bloc: Molotov Plan," *U.S. News & World Report*, 30 January 1948, 21. *St. Louis Globe-Democrat*, 18 February 1948.

Not all of Washington expected the coup. Even President Truman wrote that it looked like a repeat of 1938. Isaacson and Thomas, *The Wise Men*, 439. An article in the 25 February 1948 *San Francisco Chronicle* noted that American officials were surprised at the takeover.

136. *New York Times*, 4 May 1947, 11 May 1947, 24 February 1948, 29 February 1948; *San Francisco Chronicle*, 1 February 1948; *Chicago Tribune*, 24 January 1948.

137. Eduard Mark, "The War Scare of 1946 and Its Consequences," *Diplomatic History* 21 (Summer 1997): 415.

CHAPTER 4

1. The "normalization" of Czechoslovakia meant a return to orthodox Marxism-Leninism, total control by the Communist party, and complete subservience to the Soviet Union.

2. Klement Gottwald, the leader of the Communist party in Czechoslovakia and prime minister in 1948, engineered the 1948 coup.

3. Edward Taborsky, *Communism in Czechoslovakia, 1948–1960* (Princeton: Princeton University Press, 1961), 44-67.

4. Galia Golan, *The Czechoslovak Reform Movement: Communism in Crisis, 1962–1968* (Cambridge: Cambridge University Press, 1971), 300–302.

5. Paul Ello, comp., *Dubcek's Blueprint for Freedom: His Original Documents Leading to the Invasion of Czechoslovakia* (London: Kimber, 1969), 73–84.

6. Paul Ello, comp., *Czechoslovakia's Blueprint for "Freedom:" "Unity, Socialism, Humanity;" Dubcek's Statements, the Original and Official Documents leading to the Conflict of August, 1968* (Washington D.C.: Acropolis Books, 1968), 102–03.

7. Gordon H. Skilling, *Czechoslovakia's Interrupted Revolution* (Princeton: Princeton University Press, 1976), 412–50.

8. Golan, 279–83.

9. Ello, *Czechoslovakia's*, 122.

10. Golan, 297.

11. Ibid., 186–99.

12. In Table I the overall number of articles for the *New York Times* is approximate because of the near impossibility of counting the number of indexed articles. The method for calculation entailed counting the number of articles in one column and then multiplying by the number of columns. The small print and number of pages of references made any other procedure unworkable.

13. *New York Times*, 6 January 1968.

14. Ibid., 25 March 1968.

15. *Wall Street Journal*, 17 April 1968.

16. *New York Times*, 20 July 1968.

17. Ibid., 16 May 1968.

18. *Wall Street Journal*, 24 July 1968.

19. *Christian Science Monitor*, 20 July 1968.

20. *Wall Street Journal*, 21 August 1968.

21. *Christian Science Monitor*, 22 August 1968.

22. Ibid., 24 August 1968.

23. Ibid., 26 August 1968.

24. *New York Times*, 24, 25 August 1968.

25. Ibid., 13 August 1968.

26. Ibid., 27 August 1968.

27. *Wall Street Journal*, 13 September 1968.

28. *Christian Science Monitor*, 30 September 1968.

29. *New York Times*, 24 September 1968.

30. Ibid., 10, 13, 26 September 1968.

31. Ibid., 16 December 1968.

32. *Christian Science Monitor*, 27 December 1968.

33. *Wall Street Journal*, 18 November 1968.

34. *New York Times*, 1 December 1968.

CHAPTER 5

1. The "normalization" of Czechoslovakia meant a return to orthodox Marxism-Leninism, total control by the Communist party, and complete subservience to the Soviet Union.

2. J. F. Brown, *Eastern Europe and Communist Rule* (Durham, NC: Duke University Press, 1988), 294-315.

3. Janusz Bugajski, *Czechoslovakia: Charter 77's Decade of Dissent* (New York: Praeger, 1987), 12-17.

4. John F. N. Bradley, *Czechoslovakia's Velvet Revolution* (Boulder, CO: East European Monographs, 1992), 29-52.

5. Martin Krupa, "Transformation of Ownership in Czechoslovakia," *Soviet Studies* 44:2 (1992):297-311.

6. Carol Skalnik-Leff, *The Czech and Slovak Republics: Nation Versus State* (Boulder, CO: Westview Press, 1997), 75-125.

7. Bradley, 107-25.

8. *New York Times Index, 1989–1992.*

9. Michael G. Roskin, *The Rebirth of East Europe*, 3rd ed. (Upper Saddle River, NJ: Prentice Hall, 1997), 126-47.

10. David S. Mason, *The Rise and Fall of Communism and the Cold War* (Boulder, CO: Westview Press, 1992), 160-63.

11. *Wall Street Journal*, 16, 17 January 1989.

12. *New York Times*, 22 February 1989; *Wall Street Journal*, 22, 23 February, 10 March.

13. *Wall Street Journal*, 13 March 1989.

14. Ibid., 18 May 1989.

15. *Christian Science Monitor*, 16 June 1989.

16. *Atlanta Journal-Constitution*, 3 October 1989.

17. *Christian Science Monitor*, 27 November 1989.

18. *USA Today*, 27, 29 November 1989.

19. *New York Times*, 28 November 1989.

20. *Washington Post*, 28 November 1989.

21. *Boston Globe*, 22–27 November 1989.

22. *Chicago Tribune*, 27-29 November 1989.

23. *Atlanta Journal-Constitution*, 21–29 November 1989.

24. *Los Angeles Times*, 26 November 1989.

25. *Christian Science Monitor*, 4 December 1989.

26. *Wall Street Journal*, 1 December 1989.

27. *Washington Post*, 11 December 1989.

28. *Los Angeles Times*, 1, 3, 4, 5, 8, 9 December 1989.

CHAPTER 6

1. Permission fees covered in part by a grant from the Charles R. and Martha N. Fulton School of Liberal Arts, Salisbury University.

BIBLIOGRAPHY

Monographs

Almond, Gabriel. *The American People & Foreign Policy*. New York: Frederick A. Praeger, 1963.

Aronson, James. *The Press and the Cold War*. Indianapolis: Bobbs-Merrill Co., 1970.

Ash, Timothy Garton. *The Magic Lantern: The Revolution of 89 Witnessed in Warsaw, Budapest, Berlin and Prague*. New York: Random House, 1990.

Boyd-Barrett, Oliver. *The International News Agencies*. London: Constable, 1980.

Brown, J. F. *Eastern Europe and Communist Rule*. Durham: Duke University Press, 1988.

Cohen, Bernard. *The Press & Foreign Policy*. Princeton: Princeton University Press, 1963.

Commanger, Henry Steele and Milton Cantor, eds., *Documents of American History: Volume II Since 1898*. 10th edition. Englewood Cliffs, NJ: Prentice Hall, 1988.

Farnham, Barbara Rearden. *Roosevelt and the Munich Crisis: A Study of Political Decision-Making*. Princeton: Princeton University Press, 1997.

Fenby, Jonathan. *The International News Services*. New York: Schocken, 1986.

The Flow of the News: A Study. Zurich: International Press Institute, 1953.

Fielding, Raymond. *The March of Time, 1935–1951*. New York: Oxford University Press, 1978.

Gallup, George. William P. Hansen and Fred L. Israel, eds. *The Gallup Poll: Public Opinion 1935–1971.* New York: Random House, 1972.

Gans, Herbert J. *Deciding What's News: A Study of CBS Evening News, NBC Nightly News, Newsweek & Time.* New York: Pantheon, 1979.

Gitlin, Todd. *The Whole World Is Watching: Mass Media in the Making & Unmaking of the New Left.* Berkeley: University of California Press, 1980.

Golan, Galia. *The Czechoslovak Reform Movement: Communism in Crisis, 1962–1968.* Cambridge: Cambridge University Press, 1971.

———. *Reform Rule in Czechoslovakia: The Dubček Era 1968–1969.* Cambridge: Cambridge University Press, 1973.

Harsch, Joseph C. *Does Our Foreign Policy Make Sense?* New York: Foreign Policy Association, 1948.

Hess, Stephen. *International News & Foreign Correspondents.* Washington, D.C.: The Brookings Institution, 1996.

Isaacson, Walter and Evan Thomas. *The Wise Men: Six Friends and the World They Made.* New York: Simon & Schuster, 1986.

Kennan, George F. *Memoirs: 1925–1950.* Boston: Little, Brown and Company, 1967.

Lud'a Klusáková, ed., *Obraz druhého v historické perspektivě* (The Image of the Second in Historical Perspective). Prague: Univerzita Karlová, 1997.

Kofsky, Frank. *Harry S. Truman and the War Scare of 1948: A Successful Campaign to Deceive the Nation.* New York: St. Martin's Press, 1995.

Leff, Carol Skalnik. *The Czech and Slovak Republics: Nation Versus State.* Boulder, CO: Westview Press, 1997.

Liebovich, Louis. *The Press and the Origins of the Cold War, 1944–1947.* New York: Praeger, 1988.

Lippmann, Walter. *Public Opinion.* New York: Harcourt, Brace and

Co., 1922; reprint, The Free Press, 1965.

Lukes, Igor. *Czechoslovakia between Stalin and Hitler: The Diplomacy of Edvard Beneš in the 1930s.* New York: Oxford University Press, 1996.

Radomír Luža, *The Transfer of the Sudeten Germans: A Study of Czech-German Relations, 1933–1962.* New York: New York University Press, 1964.

MacKuen, Michael B. and Steven L. Coombs. *More Than News: Media Power in Public Affairs.* Beverly Hills, CA: Sage, 1981.

Mason, David S. *Revolution and Transition in East-Central Europe.* Second Edition. Boulder, CO: Westview Press, 1996.

Michálek, Slavomír. *Prípad Oatis: Československý komunistický režim versus dopisovateľ Associated Press* (The Oatis Case: The Communist Regime Versus the Associated Press Correspondent). Bratislava: Ústav pamäti národa, 2005.

Mlynář, Zdeněk. *Nightfrost in Prague: The End of Humane Socialism.* New York: Karz Publishers, 1980.

N. W. Ayer and Son's American Newspaper Annual and Directory. Philadelphia: N. W. Ayer and Son, 1938.

Popkin, Jeremy D., ed. *Media & Revolution: Comparative Perspectives.* Lexington: University Press of Kentucky, 1995.

Roskin, Michael G. *The Rebirth of East Europe*, Third Edition. Upper Saddle River, New Jersey: Prentice Hall, 1997.

Schmidt-Hartmann, Eva and Stanley B. Winters, eds. *Grossbritannien, die USA und die böhmischen Länder 1848–1938/Great Britain, the United States, & the Bohemian Lands 1848–1938.* Munich: R. Oldenbourg Verlag, 1991.

Schramm, Wilbur. *Mass Media and National Development.* Stanford, CA: Stanford University Press, 1964.

———. *One Day in the World's Press.* Stanford, CA: Stanford University Press, 1960.

Shoemaker, Pamela J. *Gatekeeping.* Newbury Park, CA: Sage, 1991.

Bibliography

Smith, Tony. *Foreign Attachments: The Power of Ethnic Groups in the Making of American Foreign Policy.* Cambridge, MA: Harvard University Press, 2000.

Stevenson, Robert L. and Donald L. Shaw, eds. *Foreign News & the New World Information Order.* Ames, IA: Iowa State University Press, 1984.

Sudoplatov, Pavel and Anatoli. *Special Tasks: The Memoirs of An Unwanted Witness, A Soviet Spymaster.* Boston: Little, Brown and Company, 1994.

Taborsky, Edward. *Communism in Czechoslovakia 1948–1960.* Princeton, New Jersey: Princeton University Press, 1961.

Tuchman, Gaye. *Making News: A Study in the Construction of Reality.* New York: The Free Press, 1978.

UNESCO. *Many Voices, One World.* Paris: UNESCO, 1980.

U.S., Department of Commerce, Bureau of the Census, *Historical Statistics of the United States: Colonial Times to 1970. Part 1.* Washington D.C.: Government Printing Office, 1975.

Wheaton, Bernard and Zdeněk Kavan. *The Velvet Revolution.* Boulder, CO: Westview Press, 1992.

Wightman, Gordon. "The Czech and Slovak Republics," in Stephen White, Judy Batt and Paul G. Lewis, eds., *Developments in East European Politics.* Durham: Duke University Press, 1992.

Indices

The Atlanta Journal-Constitution Index, Volume X, 1989.

The Boston Globe Index, Volume VII, 1989.

Chicago Tribune Index, Volume VIII, 1989.

Index of the Christian Science Monitor International Daily Newspaper, Volume 9, 1968.

The Christian Science Monitor Index, Volume XLV, 1989.

Los Angeles Times Index, Volume VI, 1989.

Bibliography

The New York Times Index: A Book of Record, 1968.

The New York Times Index: A Book of Record, 1989.

Readers' Guide to Periodical Literature: An Author and Subject Index
July 1937–June 1939

USA Today Index, Volume VIII, 1989.

The Washington Post Index, Volume 1, A-L, 1989.

The Wall Street Journal General News, 1968.

The Wall Street Journal General Index, 1989.

Journals
Annals of the American Academy of Political and Social Science

Communication Research

Critical Studies in Mass Communication

Current Biography: Who's News and Why 1943

Current History

Diplomatic History

East Central Europe

Editor and Publisher

Forum

Gazette

Independent Woman

IPI Report

Journal of Communication

Journal of Peace Research

Journalism & Mass Communication Quarterly

Journalism Bulletin

Journalism Quarterly

Life

Nation

National Republic

New Republic

New Yorker

Newsweek

Political Communication

Public Opinion Quarterly

Reader's Digest

Reports & Papers in Mass Communication

Saturday Evening Post

Time

U.S. News & World Report

The World Almanac and Book of Facts for 1949

Newspapers
Atlanta Constitution

Atlanta Journal-Constitution

Austin American

Austin Statesman

Baltimore Sun

Boston Globe

Chicago Daily News

Chicago Tribune

Christian Science Monitor

Evening Bulletin (Philadelphia, Pennsylvania)

Honolulu Advertiser

Bibliography

Los Angeles Times

New Orleans Times-Picayune

New York Times

Pittsburgh Courier (Pittsburgh, Pennsylvania)

Salisbury Times (Salisbury, Maryland)

St. Louis Globe-Democrat

St. Louis Post-Dispatch

San Francisco Chronicle

USA Today

Wall Street Journal

Washington Post

CONTRIBUTORS

GREGORY C. FERENCE, Professor and Graduate Director, Department of History, Salisbury University, Maryland.

OWEN V. JOHNSON, Associate Professor of Journalism and Adjunct Professor of History, Indiana University, Bloomington.

A. PAUL KUBRICHT, Professor of History and Chair of the Department of History and Political Science, LeTourneau University, Texas.

JAMES W. PETERSON, Professor and Head, Department of Political Science, Valdosta State University, Georgia.

INDEX

Index

Index

H

Harsch, Joseph C., 13–14
Havas, 4
Havel, Václav, 3, 97, 105, 109, 111
Havlíček, Karel, 60
Hayek, Jiří, 88
Henlein, Konrad, 23–24
Herblock, 18, 119, 133, 136
Hester, Al, 6
Hitler, Adolf, 2, 13, 21, 24, 26–28, 30–31,
     33–36, 39–46, 48–51, 53–54, 61–62,
     68, 113, 115, 116, 119, 120, 121, 128,
     133, 139–40
Hodža, Milan, 39
Honolulu Advertiser, 11, 22–24, 26, 30,
     33, 36, 41, 43, 46
Hoover, Herbert, 42
Horthy, Miklós, 23
Hull, Cordell, 29, 38, 44–46
Humphrey, Hubert H., 89–90
Hungary/Hungarians, 8, 23, 34, 39, 65,
     76, 78, 87, 97, 105–6, 111, 121, 128,
     131, 135– 136, 138. *See also* Austria-
     Hungary
Hur, Kyoon, 7
Husák, Gustav, 77, 95, 106, 109, 111

I

Independent Woman, 11, 22, 25, 40, 50
International Association for Mass Com-
     munications Research, 6
International Press Institute, 5
Ireland, 17
Italy, 40, 43–44, 50–52, 68–69

J

Jabulka, Jan, 23
Jakeš, Miloš, 95, 106, 108–9, 111
Japan, 23–24, 27, 32, 47, 50
Johnson, Lyndon B., 11, 78–79, 85–87,
     89, 94

K

Kádár, János, 87
Kaltenborn, H.V., 7
Kansas City, 42

Karlovy Vary, 87
Karlsbad Program, 23–25
Kennan, George F., 13, 57
Kennedy, John F., 18
Kennedy, Joseph P., 22–23, 28–29
Khrushchev, Nikita, 128, 131
Kiesinger, Kurt, 91
Kiev, 91
Kohn, Hans, 60
Korea, 14, 120, 121
Kosygin, Alexei, 84
Kuznetsov, Vasili V., 89

L

Lawrence, David, 62, 68–69
League of Nations, 49–51
Lenárt, Jozef, 83
Lewis, Flora, 3
Life, 11, 22, 26–27, 30–31, 33, 35, 39, 46,
     56, 62
Ligachev, Yegor, 105
Lippmann, Walter, 18
Locarno Treaty, 38
London, 28, 35, 38, 42
London Times, 30
Lore, Ludwig, 40–41
Los Angeles Times, 3–4, 17, 22, 24, 27,
     30–32, 35–37, 39, 41, 43, 46, 48,
     99–100, 102, 104, 108, 110
Louis XIV, 27
Louisiana, 24, 38

M

MacKenzie, DeWitt, 60
Manchuria, 50, 120, 121
March of Time, 21
Marseilles, 27
Marshall, George C., 13, 71
Marshall Plan, 12–13, 56–57, 67–70, 72,
     140
Masaryk, Jan, 13, 55, 57–58, 60, 62–63,
     65–66, 70–72, 83, 124, 125
Masaryk, Thomas G., 9, 13, 38, 60, 63,
     83, 91, 124, 127, 139
McCormick, Anne O'Hara, 27–28
McCormick, Robert R., 28

Index

Index